Praise for
Surviving the Teenage Hormone Takeover

"Having four daughters, I know ages 12-16 can be a nightmare for moms. Dr. Jackson offers wise and experienced advice on how to survive this stage through both lifestyle/psycho-spiritual guidance and the critical role of natural hormone balancing. Although she is twenty years ahead of most physicians, you and your daughter(s) don't have to wait. Here's how you can reclaim your lives, NOW!"

Jacob Teitelbaum, MD
Author of *Pain Free 1-2-3* and
Medical Director of the Fibromyalgia and Fatigue Centers of America

"Hormone specialist, Nisha Jackson, guides moms and teens with medically sound advice and caring, practical help. This is the perfect survival guide to help regain control during the teen hormone takeover. I highly recommend this book!"

Carrie Carter, MD
Author of *A Woman's Guide to Good Health* and
Columnist for *MOMSense* magazine

"This book will be greatly appreciated by practitioners and patients alike. It is a wealth of practical information and tools in an efficient, well-organized, and easy-to-understand format. My only regret is that it wasn't published in time for my family's teenage years! Thank you Dr. Jackson!"

Jim Paoletti
Director of Continuing Education
Professional Compounding Centers of Amercia

"This is a complete 21st century survival guide for young women and their families. I highly recommend it!"

Julia Ross, MA
Author of *The Mood Cure* and *The Diet Cure*

SURVIVING
THE TEENAGE
HORMONE
TAKEOVER

NISHA JACKSON, PhD
WITH MARY KORBULIC

W PUBLISHING GROUP
A Division of Thomas Nelson Publishers
Since 1798

www.wpublishinggroup.com

Published by W Publishing Group, a division of Thomas Nelson, Inc., P.O. Box 141000, Nashville, Tennessee 37214.

W Publishing Group books may be purchased in bulk for educational, business, fund-raising, or sales promotional use. For information, please email SpecialMarkets@ThomasNelson.com.

Library of Congress Cataloging-in-Publication Data

Jackson, Nisha.
    Surviving the hormone takeover / Nisha Jackson.
      p. cm.
    ISBN 0-8499-1312-8
    1. Teenage girls—Health and hygiene. 2. Teenage girls—Physiology. 3. Hormones—Psychological aspects. 4. Mothers and daughters. I. Title.
    RJ144.J33 2006
    613.9'55—dc22

2006005733

Printed in the United States of America

06 07 08 09 10 RRD 10 9 8 7 6 5 4 3 2 1

This book is dedicated to my two daughters, Jordan and McKenzie, who are cherished gifts from God. You both make me a better person every day and I love you beyond description. Thank you.

CONTENTS

ACKNOWLEDGMENTS

I thank my colleagues at Ventana Wellness Clinic and the Medford Women's Clinic for their encouragement and support in bringing this book to life. Your friendship and wisdom have been invaluable.

I am indebted to Mary Korbulic, my right-hand writer, who has adopted my love for helping women and girls and who so carefully and wonderfully breathed life into this book. I am quite sure it would not be available to the moms and teens who need it were it not for you. Thank you for your energy, love and expertise. You are the best!

Thank you to my agent, Janet Kobobel Grant, for helping me get to a place where this book could come alive and into the hands of those who need it the most. And thank you to Debbie Wickwire, Kate Etue, and Adria Haley, the adroit editors at W Publishing whose expertise helped to fine tune the manuscript.

I am so thankful to my patients who have taught me the most about caring, listening, and learning about women and their unique needs. I know without a doubt that your support, honesty and desire to get better have instilled in me a love for what I do everyday. Thank you for being my patients.

I would also like to thank my family. I have the best parents on this earth and am blessed by never-ending encouraging support and their desire to see me "do more". I have a Nana that, to this day, is one of the strongest females that ever lived. I can only hope that my determination and love of life will be as strong as yours still is. Thank you, Nana, for teaching me to love life. My late grand-parents, Marie and Lloyd, instilled in me at a very young age a desire to help others and myself with natural medicine. Vitamins, minerals, and herbal therapies were a way of life for them and I am grateful that they showed me the way so that today my patients, family, and friends have better choices for vibrant health.

To my husband, Rick—a super father, husband, and friend. I know that you didn't sign up for such a crazy ride, but I love being your wife and friend. You inspire me to be a better woman every day. Jordan and Kenzie, thank you for being my best fans. I love that you love what I do. I pray everyday that your journey through the teen years will be filled with joy, learning, love, good decisions, healthy choices, and the desire to make the most of your lives.

INTRODUCTION

TEENS—THEIR HORMONES (AND THEIR MOTHERS)

What images spring to mind as you read that title? Mothers and daughters at one another's throats? Mothers yelling, pleading, or demanding, and girls covering their ears? Girls slamming doors? Mothers tearing out their hair?

Being a teen today isn't easy. Being a teen's mom is no picnic either. As I wrote this book, colleagues and friends asked, "Why teen girls? Why their mothers?" I responded, "Why not? If anyone needs vital information about attaining hormonal health and balance, it is teen girls; and who can guide them to this information better than their mothers—the primary females with whom they share physical and emotional space?"

That's the short answer. The longer one is more complicated. It has to do with fifteen years of treating teen patients, and their mothers, in my women's health-care and hormone specialty practice. I have seen frustrated and fearful mothers, with overwhelmed and sometimes nearly defeated daughters, who have teen health problems that are becoming increasingly common. These problems include obesity, depression, eating disorders, early puberty, menstrual difficulties, and other hormone-related troubles.

I am passionate about steering teens toward the right choices regarding nutrition, exercise, stress management, medications, supplements, and sexuality. Hormone balancing in the teen years is all about back-to-the-basics common sense and rarely about taking prescription medications. It is about using information that can help prevent or overcome physical and emotional challenges. It is about knowledge I wish I had had during my own rocky and tremulous adolescence, years you could not pay me to repeat. Had I only known then what I know now about staying balanced physically and emotionally, I could have spared myself a great deal of grief.

As a gynecological health-care provider, I often find myself in the role of counselor and educator, guiding girls toward better lifestyle decisions and educating both moms and daughters. *Surviving the Teen Hormone Takeover* offers easy-to-understand principles and specific guidelines that I know to be effective. I have seen teens, most often with the help of an involved and committed parent, apply the basic principles set forth in my book, and, as a result, overcome physical or emotional difficulties to experience happier, healthier, and more hormonally balanced lives. Their moms were happier, too.

As this book goes to print, one of my daughters is a young teen and the other is on the cusp of adolesence. I fully intend to follow my own advice as I take an active parenting role during their formative teen years, which I hope will be fabulous. I know that if my daughters and I are like most mothers and daughters, we'll face hurdles and endure periods of miscommunication or uneasy silence, but we will overcome them. Like other teens, my girls will face difficult lifestyle decisions and challenging personal choices, the results of which will reverberate into adulthood. I want to be there for them, as I know you want to be there for your daughters. I thank my patients for demonstrating that knowledgeable, caring mothers can be effective coaches and teachers as they help their teens navigate puberty and adolescence.

It is my hope that mothers and daughters alike will find this book an accommodating and encouraging handbook for a more hormonally balanced and joyful journey.

1

TEENS TODAY— WHY THEY STRUGGLE

A heavyset teen girl in a midriff–baring top marched up to her mom in the checkout line and flung a bag of candy into the overflowing shopping cart. The mom removed the bag and pressed it firmly into her daughter's hands.

"No," the mom said resolutely. "We've talked about this."

"Fine!" The daughter snapped. "I'll just buy it myself then!" And off she stomped to the ten-items-or-less line, digging for change in her snug jeans.

Clearly embarrassed, the girl's mother put her hand to her forehead as the woman behind her tapped her on the shoulder.

"I have the same battle with my daughter," the second mom confided. "I try to get her to eat right, but she won't listen. She's overweight and unhappy, and I don't know what to do."

As a wave of understanding passed between them, they fell into an impassioned discussion of the joys and perils (mostly perils) of raising teen daughters in a culture adrift in empty calories, shameless sexuality, and chronic stress. Their eagerness to communicate made me realize how isolated moms can feel when things go haywire at home. I know from my medical practice how widespread their concerns are, but these two connected as if they were the only moms on earth whose daughters were troubled.

They continued to commiserate as the line inched forward, and as the first mom headed toward the parking lot, her parting comment had more than one person in line nodding in agreement. She said, "Things sure weren't like this when we were teens!"

How right she was. I held my tongue but wanted to shout, "Yes, the world is different now! But we moms don't have to abandon our daughters to the craziness of our culture. We can help them grow up healthy and strong with the knowledge and will to make good choices. We're all in this together!"

If your daughter is miserable and hurting, if she is struggling with weight, depression, chronic stress, early puberty, an eating disorder, polycystic ovary syndrome (PCOS), promiscuity, or something else that is bringing her down, don't despair. You are definitely not alone.

Every week desperate moms searching for answers bring their hurting teens to my medical office. I tell them that their daughters are not hopeless cases, and that we can work together to correct the hormonal imbalances and harmful habits that so often underlie their problems. I also tell them it may not be simple, because today's teens face challenges that their moms likely did not.

TIMES HAVE CHANGED

Being a teen girl today is not like it was two or three decades ago. True, some things remain the same. Sweet little girls have always disappeared into sometimes-prickly young women. Teen hormones have always bubbled and stewed, creating a paradox of sweet and sour, push and pull, hold on and let go. Teens today are as apt to run into the same predictable emotional and physical challenges of growing up as their mothers did. But there are more complicating factors now. To name a few:

- A pervasive fast-food and convenience culture that promotes overeating and unhealthful foods. The obesity epidemic is well-documented, and teens and youngsters are a big part of the sorry statistics.
- A shallow and exploitive pop culture that oversexualizes just about everything, especially teen girls.
- A fast-forward society steeped in stress.
- A disintegrating family structure in which the kids often get lost in the shuffle.

DID YOU KNOW?

- The age of puberty is declining, so it is not unusual for six- and seven-year-old girls to begin developing breasts and sprouting pubic hair.
- The use of antidepressant prescriptions for children increased by 50 percent between 1998 and 2002, and the use of such drugs among children grew three- to tenfold between 1987 and 1996.[1] And although FDA warnings in 2004 that antidepressants increase suicidal behavior in some children resulted in a 20 percent drop in U.S. pediatric prescriptions,[2] many doctors continue to prescribe them.
- A study of teens in fifteen industrialized countries determined that U.S. teens are the most overweight.[3]
- Eating disorders and rates of unipolar depression have soared among adolescent girls. Teen suicide has tripled.[4]

WHAT'S YOUR DAUGHTER'S DAY LIKE, REALLY?

What would it be like to be in your daughter's shoes? How does her typical day compare with your typical day twenty or thirty years ago, when you were a teen? If she is in school and pursuing the usual multitude of activities, and you are working forty hours a week, chances are you don't see her for more than an hour or two a day—and that may be stretching it. So maybe you are in the dark about what she is really thinking and doing and how she spends her time.

An informal questionnaire, included in Appendix C, reveals vast differences between what moms recall about their own lives as teens and what teens today report about their daily lives. Readers are encouraged to photocopy and complete it with their teens. If nothing else, it can generate discussion about how the world has changed. Perhaps it will raise awareness about the importance of family time and slowing down. Maybe it will open the door to talking about some of those tough issues, such as sex and personal responsibilities.

Here's what the questionnaire revealed about the moms and teens who completed it for this book.

WHAT MOMS REMEMBER—
THE "GOOD OLD DAYS"

When the moms were teens during the 1970s or '80s, their mothers cooked dinner nearly every evening, and the family spent most dinner hours together. They carried sack lunches to school. Private phone? What's that? Total phone time averaged a half hour per day, and personal computers were uncommon. Moms averaged nine hours of sleep a night as teens. They had regular chores around the house, and most began helping with cooking and cleaning as preteens. They often held part-time jobs but did not have much homework. They spent a lot of time watching television with the family, which, for the majority, included two parents. The social network revolved around the neighborhood, school, and church. They had their first date at around age sixteen and thought that about 5 percent of their peers were sexually active. Moms who were involved in athletics were rarely active in more than two sports, and practices and games were after school, not at night or on weekends. Most walked or rode bikes to get around and were not overly concerned about their weight. Most did not recall feeling constantly overburdened or stressed out.

YOUR DAUGHTER LIVES IN ANOTHER WORLD

Teen responses were about as opposite from their mothers' as you can imagine. Nearly all of the teens say that they are not assigned routine household chores, and not one said that she cooks or helps with dinner on a regular basis. Ninety percent say they spend more than two hours each day on the phone and/or the Internet. The average teen is involved with three or more extracurricular activities at any one time. Sack lunches are rare, and most teens eat in the cafeteria, or, more often, go out for fast food. (Some don't need to go off campus, however, as fast-food chains often contract with public schools.) Family dinners occur once or twice weekly, and many meals are consumed alone or in front of the television. On average, teens estimate that the family spends one uninterrupted hour a week together. All the girls who completed my survey live with their biological mothers, who are often single moms, and about half live with both their biological parents. All of the respondents who were involved in athletics play weekend games and frequently practice into the dinner hour. The teens reported averaging seven hours of sleep a night, two hours less than their mothers as teens.

Most teens who completed my questionnaire believe that about half of their peers are sexually active, and at least one of their personal friends is. The survey shows that teens have less down time and more stimuli coming at them from more directions than did their mothers. Their days are far busier, and they often feel overburdened and stressed.

WHAT WOULD YOUR TEEN SAY?

I am not suggesting that we try to force our teens to live the way we did. The world has changed, and we'll never go back. But certainly we should not forget some of the things we were doing right twenty or thirty years ago. Having downtime nurtures good health—mentally and physically. Teens assuming responsibility around the home prepares them for independence, and helping out is simply the right thing to do. Making time for family supports good mental health, encourages bonding, and gives time to bolster self-esteem in children and teens. Building awareness about how she is spending her time can help your daughter make healthier decisions and reduce her stress load. You may even see her more often! As for moms, seeing the contrast between how life was when they grew up and how life is for their daughters now may spark a reform or two in household management.

HOW TO USE THIS BOOK

This book is a resource for moms who want to guide their teens toward vibrant health and happiness in a culture that seems to thwart achieving physical, emotional, and spiritual balance. Not every chapter is for every family. The chapters on PCOS and eating disorders, for example, address very specific circumstances that apply to a relatively small percentage of teens. (When your teen is affected, however, those statistics mean zip.)

I would love to believe that every reader would devour every word of every chapter. However, moms (like their daughters) are busier than ever, and you may want to skip right to the chapters that apply to your situation. I strongly recommend, however, that you read Chapters 2, 3, 5, 7, 10, 11, and 13. Each chapter concludes with a "What Moms Can Do Today" list of practical suggestions.

2

THE TEEN
HORMONE TAKEOVER

First you have a girl skipping through childhood, seemingly unaware of boys, or of her shortcomings—if she has any. Then all of a sudden she's tucking her chin into her chest, glancing side to side, and comparing herself to magazine models and the "popular girls." In her eyes, she comes up way short. In your eyes, she's a gorgeous girl poised on the edge of womanhood. Even if most girls experience emotional and physical discomfort during the teen years, from your viewpoint, her metamorphosis into womanhood is nothing short of miraculous.

It is a hormonal happening that should be accompanied by thunderclaps—or at least drumrolls. I like to think of this amazing time as an intricate symphony scored with everything from lilting flutes to crashing cymbals—but with a lot of discordant intervals. The medical terminology describing puberty sounds dull, but when the sexual music is starting up in your daughter, it is time to listen closely. Cup your ear and you can almost hear the vibrations. Her music is going to play every month for the next several decades—approximately 450 to 480 times—and it is wise for you both to learn to understand and appreciate it.

You can do your daughter a tremendous favor by communicating to her that her body is a remarkable creation and performs incredible feats every month, all on automatic pilot. It is uplifting to be in awe of one's own body and to be tuned in as the reproductive hormones awaken and begin calling out to one another. Rather than regarding menstruation as "the curse" or "being on the rag" or some other off-putting term, girls could begin to view the presence of their monthly flow as proof that they are part of the river of life and possess great feminine power and mystery, which, of course, they do. This is not to suggest that the arrival of one's period each month should be greeted with shouts of joy, but appreciating it as a natural part of the ebb and flow of life and proof of biological soundness is a healthier approach than dreading the monthly visitation with whining or complaints, or, worst of all, shame.

The first period, called *menarche*, is actually the last hurrah of puberty, which begins two or three years earlier with the first hints of breast development. Once the periods begin, adolescence, the process of maturing after the first period, is officially under way and stretches into adulthood. From day one of the first period, a female's life is governed by the ebb and flow of hormones until she reaches menopause. (It doesn't really stop there, but that's another subject!) Menstruation is but one aspect of the maturation process, but it is an important indicator that the sex hormones have kicked in and the roller coaster is leaving the station. Hang on!

WHAT ARE HORMONES?

Hormones are incredibly potent chemical messengers that stimulate or regulate everything from metabolism to sexual development. It is impossible to overstate their fundamental role in the healthy functioning of the human body and in the normal progression from infancy through puberty and adolescence to adulthood. Endocrine glands and certain other cells produce hormones in unimaginably minute quantities but with equally astounding effects. Author Natalie Angier, in her Pulitzer prize–winning book, *Woman: An Intimate Geography*, offers this image: "You would have to drain the blood of a quarter of a million premenopausal women to obtain *one teaspoon* of estradiol, the principal estrogen of the reproductive years."[1] Yet estradiol is most responsible for transforming little girls into women.

Hormones play a role in a human life from the moment of conception. Even in the womb, the developing fetus is engaged in a complex hormonal interplay with the mother, as fetal hormones help to signal the mother's body to begin labor. The baby's hormones call to the mother, "I want out!" It isn't the last time the mother will hear her child's hormones talking.

Once the baby is born, the endocrine system is already programmed to turn hormones on and off to control metabolism, to regulate sexual development and functioning, and to spur growth at certain stages of maturation. The first two years of growth and development are dramatic, and the changes wrought by hormones during puberty are no less spectacular. Any parent who has witnessed the disappearance of his or her child into a young adult within just a few years can attest to the wonder of it all. But of course, the transformation isn't always wonderful. For some girls, puberty and adolescence are trying, tumultuous, and downright painful. As we saw in Chapter 1, puberty is starting a lot earlier for some girls, even as early as age five or six. What's going on? Before we get into the causes and complications of early puberty, let's take a look at what is considered normal development and the hormones that make it all happen.

PUBERTY AND ADOLESCENCE— THE NORMAL PROGRESSION

If you would rather skip this rather technical explanation and cut right to the chase regarding the range of normal for girls going through puberty, drop down to the box entitled "The Five Stages of Puberty" (p. 14). If you're curious about the hormonal interplay that makes the show go on every month and want to catch a glimpse of how things can go wrong, read on.

For girls, puberty usually begins quietly with the estrogen-induced enlargement of the tiny breast buds beneath the nipples. In some girls, the adrenal glands, small triangular-shaped endocrine powerhouses sitting atop the kidneys, begin pumping out adrenal hormones at about the same time. Called *adrenal androgens*, these male-type hormones include testosterone. The adrenal glands also produce the major stress hormones, adrenaline and cortisol. The adrenal glands generally mature around age ten, but as we will see below, the adrenal start-up age is declining. Testosterone stimulates pubic hair growth and, a few months later, underarm hair growth. Adrenal androgens can also create pungent underarm odor, and sometimes pimples, in both girls and boys. It is important to note that the adrenal glands have nothing to do with breast formation or menstruation. Girls may develop pubic hair years before—or after—their bodies begin showing the effects of estrogen.

In the meantime, a substance called *gonadotropin-releasing hormone* (GnRH) comes into play and sets off the chain of events awakening the ovaries into estrogen production. GnRH is made in the hypothalamus, the tiny gland above the pituitary at the base of the brain. For unknown reasons, GnRH begins to be released by the hypothalamus as the age of puberty dawns, sometime between ages seven (or even earlier these days) and thirteen. GnRH does not go into the bloodstream, but is pulsed directly to the nearby pituitary master gland, which then produces luteinizing hormone (LH) and follicle-stimulating hormone (FSH). LH, in turn, stimulates the ovaries into estrogen production, one of the ovaries' main tasks. FSH addresses the ovaries' other big job—egg production. Of course, the eggs are already present in the ovaries and have been since early in fetal development, but it is just once a month that FSH teases one egg into ripeness and coaxes it to leave its ovarian nest to brave the journey to the uterus. When that egg is en route, it morphs into the corpus luteum and pumps out a major dose of progesterone, the hormone whose primary task is to prepare the uterus to receive the fertilized egg and to sustain pregnancy, should it occur. When pregnancy does not occur, progesterone production declines sharply and triggers the shedding of the lining of the uterus in what is known as menstruation—the arrival of Aunt Flow.

The estrogens—estradiol, estrone, and estriol—are the hormones most responsible for making a girl a woman. Once bathed in estrogen, the female body truly awakens to its sexuality. Under the influence of estradiol, the most potent of the estrogens, straight-up-and-down little girls begin to change into women with curves. Breasts develop and fat accumulates in breasts and hips. The pelvis widens, and eventually menstruation begins. The process usually takes about three years, but with girls who begin puberty early, it often takes longer.

Leptin is a protein produced by fat cells. A critical level is required for puberty to progress. It is thought that once a girl's weight reaches one hundred pounds, assuming that 25 percent of her weight is fat, she is physically capable of bearing the caloric demands of carrying a child, so menstruation begins. For lack of leptin, girls who are extremely lean may not menstruate until they are sixteen or older, while overweight girls often become "teens before their time." Which leads us to the next topic.

EARLY PUBERTY

I first saw Jill when she was just seven years old and visiting my office with her mother, who was also a patient of mine. Jill's mom was concerned because Jill had developed fine pubic hair and her breasts showed signs of maturation. Jill was overweight but seemed to be a happy child—she hadn't yet realized that she was different from most girls her age. But her mother was alarmed. Would Jill start her period early? Would she develop full-fledged breasts before age ten? Would she be embarrassed because she had pubic hair? Would she attract the wrong kind of attention from older boys? Would she have to deal with the issues of adolescence before she was emotionally ready?

Those are indeed the major concerns surrounding early puberty, which has become "normal." According to a study published in *Pediatrics* in 1997, nearly half of African American girls and 15 percent of Caucasian girls begin to develop breasts and/or pubic hair by age eight. Marcia Herman-Giddens of the University of North Carolina at Chapel Hill led the study, which involved seventeen thousand girls, ages three through twelve. While the average age of the first period still hovers around twelve and one-half years for Caucasian girls and twelve years for African-American girls, youngsters are developing pubic and underarm hair and breast tissue as early as ages three and four, sometimes even earlier![2] (I don't often use exclamation points, but this fact warrants one.) Today many pediatricians are no longer alarmed when a girl shows signs of sexual development between ages six and eight. Now medical intervention to stop the development is usually done only in girls younger than six or seven, although if or when to intervene remains controversial. Why is the age of puberty dropping? Researchers hypothesize that several factors could be at play, including:

1. Obesity or overweight. Heavy girls menstruate earlier than thin girls. Remember leptin? Fat cells produce it, and when it is present in sufficient quantities, it may signal the brain that the body is ready to reproduce and it is time to initiate puberty. Overweight girls also tend to be more resistant to insulin than normal-weight girls, and their adrenal glands mature earlier. Adrenal gland maturity and pubic hair development coincide. Being too fat leads the list of probable causes of early puberty. Conversely, helping a child to maintain a healthy weight is likely the most important prevention measure.

2. Environmental chemicals that may mimic estrogen and other hormones and that have the potential to disrupt normal reproductive processes. We are literally surrounded by man-made and natural chemicals, and numerous compounds have the potential to disrupt the reproductive processes. Estrogen-like chemicals are found in many hair and beauty products and in most meat and poultry. One small study found that 8 percent of girls with early puberty had used hair care products containing estrogen-like chemicals, which can be transmitted through the skin. Endocrine disrupters include certain ubiquitous insecticides and plastics, and have been blamed for a variety of disorders, including early puberty.

3. Stress. Stress can have a pronounced effect on adrenal hormone production, and adrenal hormones stimulate the growth of pubic hair. Poor diet, lack of sleep, and inadequate exercise can worsen the effects of stress. Stress can stem from pressures at school and from peers, overloaded schedules, loss of a loved one, and parental and relationship difficulties. (see Chapter 3) Dysfunctional families, especially the lack of a father in the home and/or the presence of a stepfather or boyfriend, have been linked by separate studies to early puberty. Research in these areas continues.

So what's the problem with girls developing pubic hair and breasts in the second or third grade? As Jill's mother tearfully told me, "I don't want my little girl to be different and have the other kids make fun of her. I don't want her to get sexual attention from older boys, or to have people think she's older than she really is. I want her to have a childhood!"

Most parents of little girls who show early signs of puberty share Jill's mother's concerns. Their bodies are catapulting them into the teen world long before their childish hearts and brains are ready. People tend to think they are older than they really are and expect them to be more mature. These girls may be ostracized or teased. If they also start menstruating early, which they often do, they have a longer lifetime exposure to estradiol, increasing their breast cancer risk.

If your daughter shows signs of puberty when she is six, seven, or eight, should you worry? Clearly, early puberty is not ideal, especially emotionally and socially, but author Dr. Paul Kaplowitz, in *Early Puberty in Girls*, states: "It makes much more sense to view seven- and eight-year-old white girls and six- to eight-year-old black girls with signs of puberty as largely being healthy girls who are at the tail end of the normal distribution of the timing of puberty."[3] In other words, let's not treat these girls with drugs to stop the process.

THE FIVE STAGES OF PUBERTY

The ages at which the five stages of puberty occur have dropped overall, but the sequence of pubertal events remains the same.

1. No breast tissue enlargement or pubic hair is present. Her height will increase 2.0 to 2.4 inches a year. Ovaries are starting to enlarge, and adrenal hormones are starting to be produced.
2. A small mound of breast tissue, a breast bud, can be felt beneath the nipple, and there is a slight enlargement of the areola, the small, circular dark area around the nipple. Sparse growth of long, dark pubic hairs, straight or slightly curled, appears along the sides of the opening of the vagina. Growth accelerates to between 2.8 to 3.2 inches per year.
3. Breast tissue grows beyond the areola without contour separation. Pubic hair is darker, coarser, curlier, and spread thinly over the pubic area. Some girls get their first period late in this stage, and pimples may appear. Rapid growth can add 3.2 inches to height.
4. The areola and nipple rise above the level of the breast. Pubic hair is thicker and looks adultlike but covers a smaller area. Ovulation and menstruation usually occur but are typically irregular. Growth slows to 2.8 inches per year.
5. The girl is now physically a woman. The breasts are fully mature, with only the nipple projecting above the level of the breast. Pubic hair is distributed in an upside-down triangle and is adult in quantity and texture. Full height has been attained, and menstrual periods are well established.

HORMONES GONE AWRY—
COMMON TEEN IMBALANCES

Who hasn't heard, "Oh, she's just hormonal" when a girl is out of sorts? In many cases, this glib assessment is not far from the truth. There is no such thing as a "bad" hormone, but when hormones fluctuate abnormally or there is too much of one and not enough of another, bad things can happen. Those "bad things" may include heavy, painful periods or no periods at all, headaches, stomachaches, unstable moods, acne, weight gain, facial hair, bloating, chronic fatigue, you name it. Hormones really do play us like instruments, and it doesn't take all that much to get out of tune. If not corrected, certain hormone imbalances that begin in the teen years can lead to serious health problems down the road.

Bear in mind that it is normal for periods—and hormone levels—to fluctuate and to be irregular the first couple of years after a girl starts her period. That said, it is especially challenging for today's teens to maintain optimal hormone balance. As will be described in detail in later chapters, poor diet, sleep disturbances or deprivation, excess weight, and stress—facts of life in the United States—all contribute to the imbalances described below.

Estrogen Dominance/Progesterone Deficiency

Estrogen dominance is likely the root cause of many female health problems for women in the reproductive years, which includes teens. Whether estrogen is present in the body at excessive, medium, or low levels, if it is not balanced by progesterone, a female is said to have this condition. These two hormones balance one another to provide equilibrium in the body. For example, estrogen promotes salt and water retention, while progesterone is a natural diuretic. Estrogen makes a woman excitable, while progesterone has a calming effect. Estrogen has been associated with breast and endometrial (uterine lining) cancer, while progesterone has a cancer preventive effect.

15

What causes estrogen dominance? Most simply put, the absence or scarcity of progesterone.

Progesterone is produced primarily during ovulation. If ovulation does not occur, as it often doesn't in young teens, an imbalance results that plays a part in all the maladies listed above and more. Heavy, painful periods, cramping, weepiness, and bloating are common. When ovulation rarely or never occurs, such as when polycystic ovary syndrome is present, the poor girl is in a more-or-less constant state of estrogen dominance, which sets up further imbalances in the adrenal hormones, which can lead to obesity, acne, facial hair, chronic fatigue, and more.

INSULIN RESISTANCE

Insulin resistance is when the body does not use insulin efficiently. Not only is there plenty of the pancreas-produced hormone to go around, there is too much insulin, and certain cells are reluctant to accept it. Insulin resistance is a precursor to type 2 diabetes. Weight gain, especially around the middle, is a hallmark. While most people think *sex hormones* when referring to hormonal teens, these days they ought to think *insulin resistance* as well. Most of those young women parading their spare tires with midriff-baring or tight T-shirts are parading insulin resistance at the same time.

What causes insulin resistance? The question is answered in detail in Chapter 5. The short answer: too much sugar and refined carbohydrates and physical inactivity. The condition is part of a set of abnormalities called the metabolic syndrome.

HIGH CORTISOL LEVEL

Cortisol is an adrenal hormone that controls metabolism and regulates blood pressure and cardiovascular function, among other things. Stress can cause a spike in cortisol, which often results in less progesterone being made. This sets up a profound imbalance throughout the body. Depression, anxiety, eating disorders, headaches, stomachaches, weight gain, and sleep disturbances are among the numerous negative effects that can result.

What causes cortisol spikes? In rare instances, disease is the underlying factor. In most cases, however, garden-variety stress is the culprit. The adrenal glands react to physical and emotional stress with an outpouring of so-called stress hormones. The "hurried teen syndrome" described in Chapter 3 is so common in our culture that we rarely step back to examine the pressures that are part of our teens' day-to-day lives and protect them from the unrelenting tension that sets them up for a fall.

CORRECTING IMBALANCES

The good news is that most hormonal imbalances can be corrected, often with little more than lifestyle changes such as adequate sleep, dietary improvements, and regular exercise. Rarely do I write pharmaceutical prescriptions for teen girls, except perhaps to help a few to jumpstart in a new direction. However, I don't hold back in strongly advising teens to take advantage of these precious formative years to learn how to take care of themselves. I want them to take pleasure in the hormonal music playing within their developing bodies and singing in their youthful souls. The first lesson in achieving and maintaining hormonal health and harmony? Confront the monster stress and wrestle it into submission. Chapter 3 provides guidance.

WHAT MOMS CAN DO TODAY

1. Talk in positive language about the physical changes that are coming in your preteen or that are already well under way in your teen. Physical changes can frighten an unprepared adolescent unless she knows what to expect.
2. Provide information about puberty and adolescence. The library abounds with books on the topic if you'd rather not spend the bucks at the bookstore. And the Internet is a rich source of information.
3. Start a discussion about what you and your daughter have in common as *women*. If she is about to get her first period or has recently had this experience, tell her what it was like when you first got yours. If she is having complexion problems, chances are so did you. Does she get PMS? Do you?

3

STRESSED OUT—
WHAT ARE WE DOING
TO OUR TEENS?

McKenzie, sixteen, is a standout basketball player and a 3.9 GPA student. A member of her high school debate team, teen director of her church youth group, student government officer, and year-round competitive athlete, McKenzie has a resumé that will dazzle college scholarship committees—unless she crashes and burns first. She is so overextended that she rarely has a breather. This busy teen runs from one obligation to the next, sometimes faltering under the burden of keeping all the balls in the air at the same time. Pulling down As while taking advanced classes is challenging enough, but juggling demanding athletic practices and leadership responsibilities at the same time is over the top.

Her mother brought her to my office for a consultation. McKenzie's periods had become torrents, she was having trouble sleeping, and her mother described her episodes of snappish behavior and weepy moodiness as "very un-McKenzie-like." Obviously proud of her daughter, the concerned mom spoke glowingly of McKenzie's amazing academic and athletic accomplishments, but the girl was paying a price.

I learned that McKenzie averaged six hours of sleep per night, felt tired by midday, and had frequent stomach pains. She ate on the run, frequently indulging her taste for sweets and junk food, and was having trouble staying focused. McKenzie was clearly overextended and suffering the physical and emotional symptoms of stress. Sadly, her mother was part of the problem. She wanted desperately for her daughter to excel in all of the opportunities that she, the mother, had never enjoyed, adding to the pressure McKenzie already felt from her extreme schedule. The mother admitted that she could not imagine herself, even as a mature woman, handling all that was expected of her daughter. If you have ever thought this about your own child, perhaps it is time to step back and reevaluate. Can a schedule that demands nonstop mental and physical hustle be healthy at any age?

McKenzie's lab tests revealed that her progesterone level just before her period was low and probably the cause of her heavier flows. Her estrogen was at the high end of normal, most likely promoting the negative moodiness and cravings associated with premenstrual syndrome (PMS). Considering the crazy pace of her life, her imbalances didn't come as a surprise.

CHRONIC STRESS HAMMERS BODY AND SOUL

The funny thing about stress is that when taken in small to moderate doses, it can be beneficial. It keeps us on our toes and helps us to meet deadlines and challenges with physical and mental alertness. Stress becomes toxic when it is chronic, and the Centers for Disease Control and Prevention (CDC) estimate that up to 90 percent of doctor visits in the United States may be stressrelated.[1] Teens who are juggling homework, boyfriends, the social pecking order, work, family dynamics, and more are often suffering from stress-caused adrenal overload and the resulting hormonal havoc.

The adrenal glands are small triangular-shaped chemical factories perched atop the kidneys. These glands regulate metabolism, produce reproductive hormones, and are the primary sources of the stress hormones—adrenaline and cortisol. Adrenaline produces the big-guns stress reaction. Called the fight-or-flight response, it is nothing short of amazing. In an instant—say you're about to be run over by a truck—the adrenal glands fire adrenaline into your system. The pupils dilate, allowing more light to enter the eye; stored sugars and fats pour into the blood to provide fuel for quick energy; and the breathing rate escalates to provide more oxygen. Red blood cells flood the bloodstream, carrying more oxygen to the muscles and the brain. The heart rate increases and blood pressure soars. Blood-clotting mechanisms are activated to protect against injury, and muscles tense in preparation for whatever may come. Digestion shuts down, and blood is diverted to the muscles and brain. Perspiration and salivation increase.

Your daughter will rarely experience any true fight-or-flight, live-or-die situations. However, her stress response to giving a speech, taking a test, or suddenly seeing that cute guy she has a mad crush on can make her heart thump and her palms sweat with nearly the same intensity as if she were being pursued by a teen-eating tiger. The body is built to handle occasional adrenaline bursts. Chronic tension, on the other hand, spurs the adrenals to produce a more-or-less steady pulse of stress hormones, which, over time, take a physical and emotional toll. Chronic stress produces the keyed-up, on-edge tension that can lead to what I call "brain fade." That's when concentration is cluttered, you forget everything you studied or practiced, and your stomach hurts. If you're taking a test or giving a speech, you're sunk. Teens who learn to reduce stress can avoid brain fade, sleeplessness, depression, and the other negative effects of unrelenting tension. What's more, they have a good shot at carrying their stress-management skills into the future, where the need to juggle personal, professional, and family responsibilities is a given.

GETTING STRESS UNDER CONTROL

In McKenzie's case, relieving her physical and emotional symptoms gave her a jump-start on subduing stress for the long haul. I prescribed the monthly use of over-the-counter evening primrose oil (EPO) to help relieve her PMS, and two months of plant-based bioidentical progesterone to improve her estrogen/progesterone balance. Natural progesterone, available by prescription through compounding pharmacies,[2] or, in weaker concentrations, over-the-counter progesterone, was prescribed rather than birth-control pills—a common remedy for excessive menstrual flow—because it corrects the underlying problems rather than masks the symptoms.

On the activity-overload side, McKenzie agreed to the following:

- ◻ Ditch at least two activities in her schedule, giving her more time to concentrate on her priorities: schoolwork and basketball.
- ◻ Just say no to any additional obligations unless she traded out something already on her weekly roster.
- ◻ Get at least eight hours of sleep nightly.
- ◻ Arise early to complete homework, if necessary.
- ◻ Take time every day to close her eyes, take a few deep breaths, and relax.

McKenzie learned how to tame stress, and if she's smart, she will hang on to those lessons as she matures. Getting enough rest, taking time for herself, exercising, eating right—these are basics that we need to constantly review to avoid lapsing into the hamster syndrome—frantically charging around the treadmill in our little cages of have-to-dos.

McKenzie also had nutritional counseling, which was every bit as important as reducing her activities and regulating her female hormones. (See Chapter 6 for tips on eating for life.) She learned that she needed more complete protein and fewer refined carbohydrates, and she agreed to pay better attention to nutrition. By her follow-up visit three months later, McKenzie's stomachaches had resolved and she was feeling happier and more emotionally stable. Her periods had returned to normal and the PMS symptoms had all but disappeared. Her sugar cravings were diminished, and she noticed that she had better concentration and mental focus. She had also dropped five pounds.

EFFECTS OF STRESS OVERLOAD

- Depression
- Headaches
- Stomachaches
- Eating disorders
- Alcohol or drug use
- Anxiety
- Exhaustion
- Moodiness
- Lack of motivation, inertia
- Sugar and carbohydrate cravings
- Fatigue
- Weight gain, especially around the middle
- Sleep problems
- Menstrual difficulties
- Irritability
- Rage

TOXIC STRESS BEGINS EARLY

McKenzie came by her stress-related symptoms honestly. Her induction into the world of too many demands began when she started piano and dance lessons at age six and escalated from there. Depending upon the season, she was also enrolled in so-called recreational league soccer, basketball, and softball teams. I often wonder which children are under the most stress on these teams. Is it the timid child who spends a disproportionate amount of time benched—despite the fact that all kids are supposed to get equal play—or girls like McKenzie, who are often expected to pull the team to victory? Either way, many youngsters are scheduled into too many organized activities that require regular practices as well as performances and games, and they have little time for free and creative play. Having one or maybe two organized activities in elementary and middle school is great, but overscheduling sets youngsters up for adrenal overload. There are significant sources of teen stress (see Common Sources of Teen Stress below) that parents can't do much about, but overscheduling is within our influence.

Unfortunately, too many adult women are themselves overburdened and reeling under the combined weight of working full-time outside as well as inside the home. They often lack the coping skills they need to help themselves, let alone to educate their daughters. These women experience significant stress-induced physical and emotional complaints and become poor role models. If Mom doesn't give herself a break and expects the same nonstop performance from her daughter, the daughter grows up believing that's the way life is supposed to be. Being chronically fatigued, depressed, angry, and resentful about having no time for yourself is no way to live.

COMMON SOURCES OF TEEN STRESS

- ☑ Problems with schoolwork and academic load
- ☐ Moving or changing schools
- ☐ Working too many hours
- ☑ Poverty
- ☐ Overloaded schedules
- ☐ Family tension, dysfunction
- ☐ Bullying
- ☑ Lack of sleep
- ☐ High-sugar diet
- ☐ Unrealistic expectations
- ☑ Lack of popularity, social acceptance, cliques
- ☑ Boys, boyfriends
- ☐ Not having the "right" clothes, possessions

- ✗ Being overweight, concerns about appearance
- ☐ Power struggles with parents, teachers
- ☒ Concerns about the future
- ☐ Divorce or separation of parents (huge stress!)
- ☐ Loss of a loved one
- ☐ Racism

MANAGING STRESS

Stress happens. Busy schedules and being overcommitted are part of our culture. There is no way for a teen—or anyone else—to completely avoid it. But observing a few simple rules can minimize the negative effects.

1. Get enough sleep. Teens need eight to nine hours every night for recovery, growth, and hormone balance. It is important for teens to be consistent with bedtimes and wake times. The body's internal clock is thrown for a loop by wild fluctuations in sleep hours, causing restlessness and fatigue. Neurochemicals necessary for clear thinking and mood stability are produced in sleep.

2. Set priorities. If your teen has too much on her plate, help her to sort out what's most important. Choose one or two of the most rewarding activities and phase out the rest. Encourage her to set aside pride, ego, and an obsession to overachieve and to take the time to enjoy life.

3. Breathe. It sounds elementary, but yoga practitioners around the world know the importance of conscious breathing. Slow, deliberate, mindful breathing sets up the relaxation response, even if practiced for just a few minutes. It reduces cortisol release, making the body less reactive to stress. Teach your daughter how to use breathing techniques to calm herself at school, work, home, in the car, wherever. Try sitting in a chair and breathe in to the count of six. Hold it for the count of three, and then exhale to the count of six.

4. Schedule time to pray, meditate, or just relax. Here's one area where scheduling is good. Without a conscious effort, taking the time to slow down might not happen. The physical response to relaxation produces chemicals that sooth the psyche. Reading a book, soaking in a hot tub, catching a short nap, spending time with a pet, temporarily doing absolutely nothing—all can ease back the stress throttle.

5. Eat right. Breakfast is the most important meal of your teen's day. She should eat at least three meals per day plus two or three healthy snacks to help with brain function and to keep her metabolism stoked.

6. Choose positive influences and develop a supportive network. As her mother, you can't choose her friends no matter how hard you try, but you can steer her toward situations and environments where she is most likely to come under positive influences. Church youth groups, community-based youth organizations, school clubs and activities, even health clubs and gyms, are likely to be loaded with the peers you'd like to see your daughter develop as buddies. Friends who are well-balanced, upbeat, and constructive can do a lot to help your daughter grow in confidence. Negative, controlling friends, on the other hand, can take an emotional toll, dragging her into unhealthy behaviors and creating more stress.

7. Exercise regularly. This is the stress reliever that works every time. If you're hooked on exercise yourself, you know that on those inevitable days when you're strung as tightly as a guitar string, a good walk or run relieves the tension. Starting from an early age, involve your daughter in organized sports, or, if she prefers, enroll her in dance, gymnastic, karate, or other lessons. (But only one or two at the same time.) Organize active family outings. Set a good example by being active yourself.

8. Say yes to optimism. We all know happy people who manage to see the glass as half full rather than half empty. One of the most significant findings in psychology in the last twenty years is that individuals can choose the way they think. Your daughter will become what she thinks, so she might as well think that she is healthy, energetic, happy, clear-minded, and in control.

9. Say no to overextension. The ability to say no takes practice and basic assertiveness training. Teach your daughter to state her feelings in a polite, firm manner. "I'm sorry, but I can't take on one more thing right now."

10. Meet challenges one step at a time—and don't be afraid to ask for help. When her to-do list is overwhelming, your daughter may throw up her hands, literally or figuratively, and become immobilized and depressed. Teach her to take control by biting off small chunks. Doing one page of her math assignment, filling out one scholarship application, organizing one corner of her room, cleaning out her book bag—all can help her to feel more in control. And let her know that it is always okay to ask for a little help from her friends—or her mom.

JUMPSTART PLAN TO BEAT STRESS

If I had to recommend just two surefire ways to beat stress every day they would be:

1. **Exercise at least five days a week.** Walking, jogging, biking, doing yoga or karate, dancing, playing tennis, doing step aerobics, walking in place in front of the television, lifting weights, using a rowing machine, skipping rope, playing hopscotch, swimming, horseback riding—whatever you want just

so long as it gets you moving. Thirty minutes a day is good, and anything more is a bonus. If your teen is involved in sports, exercise isn't such a hard sell because she has already learned how much better she feels when she's active. But if your teen is overweight, lethargic, and claims to "hate to sweat," selling her on the idea of regular exercise may be a challenge. Building an exercise habit is so important to her current state of mind and her lifelong health, however, that your persistence and creativity in getting her moving is imperative. Join her. Sign her up for a health club. Bribe her with a new cell phone. Whatever it takes. Becoming physically active will do wonders for her physical and emotional health.

2. **Eat well, starting with a good breakfast.** By "good" I mean *protein*. Sugary processed cereals, including most cold cereals, pancakes or waffles with syrup, bagels—most of the usual breakfast fare—are terrible foods to fuel her day. If she eats a carbohydrate-heavy breakfast at 7:00 a.m., she'll be hungry by 10:00 a.m., guaranteed. She'll also feel tired and edgy. Trust me. She will perform much better and handle stress more easily with eggs, meat, peanut butter, or other slow-burning protein-rich foods under her belt.

DAILY SUPPORTIVE SUPPLEMENTS TO COMBAT STRESS

□ Multivitamin with iron
□ Vitamin C: 500–1,000 mg, liquid or capsules
□ Zinc: 10–25 mg
□ B complex vitamins: under-the-tongue preparation or capsules. Use a B100 complex.

□ Omega-3 fatty acids, fish oil or flaxseed oil capsules: 1,000 mg
□ Calcium-magnesium: 500–800 mg calcium; 200–400 mg magnesium. Take in the evening.
□ Evening primrose oil capsules: 500–1,200 mg

WHAT MOMS CAN DO TODAY

1. Be a good role model. Take time for yourself.
2. Set realistic expectations. She may seem like Supergirl, but she's still a kid.
3. Respect her. Respect yourself.
4. Make yourself available to talk anytime, anyplace.
5. Invite her to go to the gym, to walk or run, or to join you in another physical activity.
6. Recognize music as a stress reliever, and don't judge her by the music she chooses.
7. Turn off the television, turn on soothing music, and light candles.
8. Enforce a reasonable bedtime.
9. Get up earlier and make a breakfast that includes protein and excludes sugar. Skip the juice.
10. Pray. Meditate. Breathe.

4

THE TEEN
MOOD MOUNTAIN

Lauren was sulking again. The fifteen-year-old was holed up in her room, *not* talking on the phone, *not* watching television, *not* tapping out an e-mail, *not* listening to music, *and not* devouring the contents of the refrigerator. She was doing nothing but lying on her bed staring at the ceiling. When her mother asked how her day went, Lauren turned toward the wall. When pressed for a response, she snarled, "Just leave me alone." She wasn't hungry at dinnertime, and when asked if she had homework, Lauren snapped, "None of your business." Later, her mom thought she heard her daughter crying. Brokenhearted, Lauren's mother endured another sleepless night wondering what was happening to her daughter.

Was her once-carefree girl experiencing normal teen angst associated with hormonal upheaval and the social, physical, emotional, and psychological changes of this roller-coaster time of life? Was she just having a bad day? Or was she seriously depressed and at risk for all the adversities that can go with it: slipping grades, loss of relationships, risky behaviors, eating disorders, and, at worst, suicide? Lauren's mother went with her gut and made an appointment for Lauren with a counselor. Good call.

Persistent withdrawal and sadness are strong indicators of serious depression, but a diagnosis depends on many other factors. Mothers and/or guardians—someone who loves a teen girl and observes her behavior and moods every day—are in a better position than anyone else, when they know the symptoms, to judge whether or not a girl needs help. What I'm telling you is *trust your instincts*. If, like Lauren's mother, you believe your daughter's bad moods are beyond what should be expected, then they probably are.

So then what? Who can help? And how? In this chapter we will explore what teen depression is and what it is not, and how it can be safely treated.

TEEN DEPRESSION ON THE RISE

According to a study conducted by the World Health Organization, The World Bank, and Harvard University, major depression is the leading cause of disability worldwide among those age five and older, and ranks second only to ischemic heart disease in creating a health burden in market economies such as the United States. The study predicts that by 2020, psychiatric and neurological conditions could increase by nearly half, from 10.5 percent of the total disease burden to almost 15 percent.[1] Twenty years ago, teen depression was almost unheard of, yet recent surveys indicate that as many as one in five teens now suffers from it.

IS IT DEPRESSION OR A BAD MOOD?

Clinical depression is definitely more than feeling sad for a day or two; it is when the blues last for weeks or months. Dismissing a girl's persistent sadness and crankiness as "just hormonal" and "normal for her age" is a mistake. Brown University reported in 2002 that many parents simply do not recognize the symptoms of depression in their adolescent children. They found that even parents who have good communication with their children do not necessarily realize it when a child is depressed. Feeling bad day after day is *not* normal! Schoolwork, energy level, behavior, social activities, weight, and the ability to bounce back are all directly impacted by depression, which can be life threatening. The startling facts:

- ▢ Suicide is the third leading cause of death for young people between ages fifteen and twenty-four, and it is the sixth leading cause of death among five- to fourteen-year-olds.[2]
- ▢ In 1996, more teenagers and young adults died of suicide than from cancer, heart disease, AIDS, birth defects, stroke, pneumonia, influenza, and chronic lung disease combined.[3]
- ▢ In the United States, more than four times as many boys die by suicide, but girls attempt suicide more often and report higher rates of depression.[4]
- ▢ A recent survey of high-school students found that almost one in five had seriously considered suicide, and more than one in six had made plans to attempt it.[5]

Depression is chillingly described in the best-selling novel *Prozac Nation: Young and Depressed in America* by Elizabeth Wurtzel.

> But depression is not a sudden disaster. It is like a cancer. At first its tumorous mass is not even noticeable to the careful eye, and then one day—wham!—there is a huge, deadly seven-pound lump lodged in your brain or your stomach or your shoulder blade, and this thing that your own body has produced is actually trying to kill you.[6]

My young patients who say they are depressed express similar feelings that some sinister presence has come to roost in their brains. Even girls who appear to have everything—looks, popularity, money, stable homes—can be seriously depressed for no apparent reason.

BEYOND ANTIDEPRESSANTS

Obviously, a teen who is immobilized by sadness needs help, and today that help often comes in the form of powerful drugs known as antidepressants, or selective serotonin reuptake inhibitors. About eleven million prescriptions for this group of newer antidepressants were written in 2002 for American children under eighteen, according to the Federal Drug Administration.[7] And until the FDA in 2005 issued a warning to doctors that prescribing antidepressants to children and teens may be linked to suicidal thinking and behavior and other forms of violence, the number of kids on antidepressants had been growing at a rate faster than any other segment of the population. This was true even though the FDA had not approved all of them for the treatment of depression, nor found them to be effective and safe for children under the age of eighteen. Despite the warnings, many primary care providers and pediatricians continue to hand out prescriptions. The fifteen-year-old perpetrator in a 2005 school shooting incident in Red Lake, Minnesota, was taking Prozac, one of the most commonly prescribed antidepressants. Numerous teen suicides have been associated with antidepressant use.

The question remains whether we should be subjecting youngsters to the potentially serious risks of these potent drugs. I think not. There is no definitive proof that antidepressant medications are safe and effective for teens—or anyone else, for that matter—and the fact that chemical changes that result from depression in children differ from chemical changes in adults makes me question why young people are being prescribed the same medications.

I can't tell you how many times I have avoided prescribing antidepressants to teens. Unless the situation seems life threatening—the teen has attempted suicide or is threatening to do so—I rarely prescribe them. Instead, the first lines of treatment include therapy, stress management, relaxation techniques, problem solving, detailed hormone testing and intervention, brain chemistry analysis, family counseling, detailed nutritional counseling, and natural supplements for balancing mood and brain chemistry.

These methods take time and energy, which patients and medical providers should expect to expend to solve complex problems. Too often patients just want the quick fix. Our society isn't okay with feeling bad. We want to get on with our busy lives as soon as possible after a divorce, the loss of a loved one, a serious accident, a move to a new home, or other life-altering events. We forget that it is perfectly normal to cry and to grieve. If you are still crying months after somebody you loved died or left you, that's normal. If your husband left the family and your daughter is still angry a year later, that's normal. Sometimes we all need help working through emotional trials, but most people are resilient and can bounce back after going through the stages of grieving and giving themselves time to heal. Love, counseling, healthy diet, adequate sleep, positive environment, therapy, supportive friends and family—all are essential ingredients to getting better. I have seen deeply troubled young people turn themselves around without rushing it with drugs.

When discussing antidepressants with mothers, either for themselves or for their teen, I explain that nearly 60 percent of those taking antidepressants experience profound changes that include a lessening of testosterone. Many parents respond by saying, "Well, that's good because I really don't care to have Suzie experiencing sexual feelings right now."

Unfortunately, diminished sexuality is just part of the story with the testosterone reduction that can occur when serotonin boosting antidepressants are used. Serotonin boosters influence the release of testosterone and sex hormone-binding globulin, as well as other important hormones that can also have an impact on the developing reproductive system. Testosterone is a misunderstood hormone in females. True, it enhances sexual desire and response, but it also boosts energy and improves strength, endurance, drive, memory, concentration, and brain function. Adequate testosterone makes girls have a greater zest for life and feel creative and spontaneous. Every teen girl who is considering taking an antidepressant needs to know that it could actually make her feel worse. These potential side effects need to be discussed with parents and teens.

TYPES OF DEPRESSION

There are two primary types of depressive illness: the sad kind, called major or clinical depression, and bipolar disorder, which used to be called manic-depressive disease. Bipolar disorder usually begins in adult life but does occur in teens and even children. It is characterized by wild mood swings from deep depression to a speeded-up, reckless state. (Many adolescents and adults also suffer from seasonal affective disorder (SAD) brought on by the gloom of winter. SAD symptoms are the same as for depression but can usually be alleviated by daily exposure to sunlight or another bright light source.)

Take a look at the following checklist for an idea of whether your daughter is hopping on and off the hormonal horse of adolescence, or if her depression is something she can't shake. Keep in mind that depressed teens may be much crankier and angrier rather than sad and weepy. *If five or more of the following symptoms last for more than two weeks, or if any of these symptoms results in major disruption in any area of life, a professional evaluation is in order.*

SYMPTOMS OF DEPRESSION

- ☐ Crying and sadness that doesn't go away.
- ☐ Feelings of guilt, loss of confidence and self-esteem.
- ☐ A feeling that life is meaningless, as if nothing good is ever going to happen again.
- ☐ Persistent negative attitude.
- ☐ Lack of feeling for anything or anyone, doesn't care.

- Loss of interest in things that used to bring pleasure, such as music, friends, sports.
- Wants to be left alone most of the time.
- Inability to concentrate, indecisiveness, forgetfulness.
- Irritability and tendency to overreact.
- Change in sleep patterns, inability to sleep, sleeping a lot more than usual, trouble falling asleep at night, waking up and not being able to get back to sleep.
- Change in eating patterns, eating a lot more or a lot less than usual.
- Exhaustion, feeling tired and restless most of the time.
- Chronic headaches and joint and muscle pains.
- Frequent stomachaches.
- Hostility, anger, and aggression out of proportion to situation.
- Preoccupation with death, expressing thoughts of suicide.

SYMPTOMS OF DEPRESSION THAT MAY BE ASSOCIATED ESPECIALLY WITH CHILDREN AND ADOLESCENTS

- Frequent vague, nonspecific physical complaints, such as headaches, muscle aches, stomachaches, or tiredness.
- Frequent absences from school or poor school performance.
- Talk of running away from home or efforts to do so.
- Outbursts of shouting, complaining, unexplained irritability, or crying.
- Boredom.
- Social isolation, poor communication.
- Extreme sensitivity to rejection or failure.

Note: Serious behavioral issues, such as sexual promiscuity, substance abuse, and eating disorders are often linked with depression.

MANIC SYMPTOMS IN BIPOLAR DISORDER

☐ Feels on top of the world, high as a kite—a nonstop party in constant motion.

☐ Has unrealistic ideas about the great things she can do that, in reality, she can't.

☐ Is extremely talkative, jumping from subject to subject.

☐ Exhibits wild behavior in driving; spending money; or with sex, drugs, or alcohol.

☐ Lack of interest in sleep and, often, inability to sleep.

☐ Irritable, rebellious, and unable to get along at home or school.

Note: The depressive symptoms of bipolar disorder are similar to those of clinical depression.

CAUSES OF DEPRESSION

No one can say for certain why some teens can shake off inevitable feelings of melancholy and regain their emotional equilibrium, while others get stuck in sadness. Family history is an important indicator for depression, but I believe that brain chemicals and hormone imbalances brought on by poor diet and chronic stress play major roles. In addition, a lack of connectedness to others and to moral and spiritual meaning isolates some young people and contributes to the growing tide of teen depression.

THE HORMONE CONNECTION

Rarely does a day go by that I don't wonder where all this depression is coming from. In my practice I have observed that more and more girls are feeling sad, chronically fatigued, emotionally unstable, and angry. I can't help but think that the insane pace of most families' lives and the increasing social, emotional, and academic pressures teens face contribute to the ballooning rate of adolescent mental health problems.

To a teen girl, a boyfriend's rejection, a peer group's shunning, a bad grade on a test, a racial slur, or a family fight are among the triggers that can produce profound despair, setting up an adrenal response that sends a cascade of the stress chemicals—adrenaline and cortisol—surging through the body. If this happens time and again, chemical and hormonal imbalances can become chronic and depression can be among the sorry results. Chronic stress also contributes to weight gain, menstrual problems, substance abuse, and inertia.

There is little doubt that depression throws a wrench into the intricate mind-body connection, and there is general agreement that certain neurotransmitters—primarily serotonin, epinephrine, and dopamine— are out of sync when a person is depressed. Neurotransmitters are chemicals used by brain cells to communicate with the rest of the body. They provide a sense of calm and emotional balance.

Some hormones and neurochemicals that can become imbalanced with depression are:

- Serotonin: Neurotransmitter and hormone thought to be responsible for emotional states, sleep, and memory. Reduced levels can lead to depression, sleep disturbances, and memory problems.
- Estrogens: Class of female hormones responsible for secondary sexual characteristics. Too much or too little can lead to emotional instability, anger, irrational behavior, and physical complaints.
- Progesterone: Mood disturbances are among the effects of reduced levels of this female hormone.
- Dopamine: Chemical compound found in the brain that transmits nerve impulses. When reduced can lead to loss of zest, inability to concentrate, and reduced mental acuity, energy, and drive.
- Endorphins: Natural mood-lifting brain chemicals that are often reduced in depression. Exercise increases endorphins.

▫ GABA: gamma-aminobutyric acid, an important amino acid neuro-transmitter in the brain. Induces relaxation and sleep.

▫ Norepinephrine: An adrenal hormone and a neurotransmitter. Changes in the norepinephrine system are implicated in depression.

THE DIET CONNECTION

Many researchers agree that a link exists between poor nutrition and depression. Amino acids, components of protein essential for overall health and brain functioning, are especially important to mood. Many of my patients have low amino acid levels, causing them to feel tired, depressed, agitated, and emotionally imbalanced.

Diets loaded with sugar and refined carbohydrates do more than make people fat. They can also make them sad. Julia Ross, author of *The Diet Cure*, says that teens who are eating mostly refined and sugary foods and getting inadequate protein will tend toward depression and anxiety.[8] This can be especially true when teens try vegetarianism. Among the first nutrients out the door with uneducated vegetarianism is tryptophan, an amino acid that occurs in proteins. Tryptophan is essential for growth and normal metabolism and is a precursor of serotonin, a chemical that acts as a calming agent in the brain and plays a role in sleep. Ross says that when you start smiling less and being more irritable, it is a sure sign of diminishing serotonin. Teens on a protein-deficient diet will ultimately lose muscle mass and experience insufficient production of brain chemicals, leading to all sorts of mood disorders.

It is amazing to see what happens when amino acid levels are restored to optimal ranges. If your teen is depressed, please read Ross's *The Mood Cure*, which explains the various amino acids and their effects on mood, emotion, memory, mental performance, and more. The amino acids and supplements I have found to be most effective in treating depression are listed later in this chapter.

FAMILY HISTORY

If anyone in the immediate family suffers from depression, the children are about six times likelier than their peers to become depressed. However, it is unclear whether the predisposition is in the genes or in long exposure to dysfunctional personal and family dynamics, which include poor anger management, low self-esteem, extreme pessimism, poor communication skills, and difficulty in coping with stress. When parents are barely coping with their own problems, it isn't surprising that they are unable to provide emotional support for their teens. Parental finger pointing and unwillingness to address their own issues can have a serious negative impact on struggling teens. In addition, researchers at the National Institutes of Health have found a link between depression and traumas experienced in early childhood. It isn't surprising that teens who were abused or neglected as children are likelier to suffer from depression.

In an ideal world parents would be healthy, well-balanced, loving, sensitive, and wise. They would have tons of time to lavish on their offspring and would realize that putting their children first is in everybody's best interest. Alas, parents are just human and have their own problems. When adults in the home are not functioning well, the kids may follow suit. Individual, group, and/or family therapy can be of utmost importance.

CHRONIC STRESS

Teens today live in a different world from their parents. The pace is faster, the demands are greater, and the pressure from teachers, friends, parents, and popular culture is unrelenting. Peer pressure is nothing new and is as influential—and stressful—as ever. But media pressure to look and act a certain way and to acquire more and more is omnipresent and insidious. There is a prevailing sense that whoever you are and whatever you have, it isn't quite good enough. In an Australian study of four hundred children ages nine to twelve, 16 were found to be clinically depressed with 112 assessed as being vulnerable to depression. The depressed children believed that happiness is achieved through the acquisition of fame, money, and beauty. Happier children tended to believe that feeling good comes from healthy attitudes and pursuing worthwhile goals.

As seen in Chapter 3, an onslaught of teen stress comes from overloaded schedules and unrealistic expectations as well as from family conflicts, racial prejudice, and on and on. As she juggles the conflicting demands of school, work, family, and her all-important social life, your teen is practicing for the hamster wheel that traps so many adult women and can lead to depression.

LACK OF CONNECTEDNESS

Children and teens who feel isolated and alone are more prone to depression and other problems and are less able to rebound from setbacks. *Hardwired to Connect,* a report issued in 2003 by the Commission on Children at Risk, a panel of leading pediatricians, research scientists, and youth service professionals, says that a lack of connectedness to others and a lack of deep connections to moral and spiritual meaning is causing a mental health crisis in American childhoods.[9]

Scientific studies cited in the report suggest that "meeting children's needs for enduring attachments and for moral and spiritual meaning" is the best way to ensure their healthy development. The report describes the powerful effects of strong nurturing on genetic transcription and brain circuitry, and offers evidence that our ability and need to become and stay attached to others is biologically programmed.

During the teen years, it is right and good that teens begin to pull away and establish themselves as independent beings. That pulling can feel more like ripping at times and can result in hurt feelings. How can it be that the sweet little girl who used to crawl into your lap, put her arms around your neck and coo, "I love you, Mommy," is now slamming the door in your face? Even as she shuts you out, continue to let her know that you are always there when she needs you.

THE TEEN BRAIN—NOT QUITE ADULT

Your daughter may look like an adult and even think she is an adult, but current research indicates that most teens have not yet developed a reasoned response to challenges and upsets. Although the brain is as large as it is going to be by age twelve or thirteen, it is not fully developed. Imaging studies conducted by Dr. Jay Giedd and colleagues at the National Institute of Mental Health indicate that the adolescent brain undergoes extensive structural changes throughout puberty and into young adulthood.[10] It isn't until after age twenty that the brain develops the "executive function," which explains why teens may be quick to react but slow to consider the consequences, and why your teen will watch television for two hours before tackling a term paper due the next day. It also helps to explain how the proverbial molehill easily attains mountain stature. From the adult perspective, losing a boyfriend or being dumped by friends seems harsh, but we know that life moves on and another love or new friends will come along. To your daughter, however, these upsets can seem like the worst thing that can possibly happen and life will never be worth living again. Usually, she *will* get over whatever is causing her distress. It's when she doesn't rebound and the depression becomes chronic that help should be sought.

SEEKING HELP

Most seriously depressed people, teens in particular, don't seek help on their own. Inertia and feelings of hopelessness are signs of depression that make taking action of any sort difficult, especially reaching out for help. If you believe your daughter needs professional evaluation, you will have to do the reaching out for her. Family medical providers, mental health specialists and counselors, and private and community health agencies exist in nearly every community. If at all possible, however, I recommend your first stop should be a hormonal or naturopathic preventive specialist who can test for and treat hormonal and nutritional deficiencies that may be at the root of the problem, or at least contributing to it. So many times in my practice I see teens whose hormonal upheavals and mood dives can be improved through stress reduction, improved nutrition, and hormone balancing.

TESTING FOR DEPRESSION

When a mother brings her teen to me and says she believes her daughter is suffering from depression, we launch a series of evaluations:

☐ Questionnaire asking the teen to evaluate her emotional state, her daily schedule, and her stress level.

☐ Lab tests to evaluate blood levels of amino acids, vitamins, and hormones, including estradiol, progesterone, testosterone, DHEA-S, serotonin, and thyroid panel.

☐ Diet evaluation, specifically looking for foods that contribute to depression—sugar, chemical additives, soft drinks, junk food, and lack of protein.

☐ Food allergies or sensitivities may be involved in mood disorders and can be tested for.

☐ Testing for neuro-brain chemical imbalance through Neuro-Relief Science Labs is helpful in identifying underlying chemistry problems and ultimately outlining the specific amino acids and supplements needed to balance brain chemistry and mood.

If you believe your teen is depressed, please start with commonsense solutions: diet, exercise, and stress reduction. With the nutrient-deficient diet that too many teens follow, it will come as no surprise that improving the diet is often the first line of treatment. Providing the amino acids found in complete proteins such as meat and eggs can go a long way toward correcting depression and mood disturbances. So can exercise. It is absolutely true that regular exercise lifts the spirits. Persuading a depressed teen to eat a nice omelet and go for a walk in the sunshine may seem too simplistic—and too hard a sell. After all, when a person is immobilized by depression, it isn't a given that she will respond in a positive way to your suggestions. In some cases, however, just the extra attention and caring can help to lift her spirits, and healthy food and a walk in the fresh air may be enough to shift her mood.

Obviously, some depressed teens need more than a walk in the park to shake deep depression. If she does not respond to, or refuses, dietary changes and exercise, counseling with a trained therapist is in order. In the meantime, don't give up on her. Keep up the efforts to communicate. Even as she pulls away, she needs those who love her more than ever in order to feel grounded and connected.

COUNSELING AND PSYCHOTHERAPY

Talk is good! But some forms of therapy work better than others. A National Institute of Mental Health–supported study that compared different types of psychotherapy for major depression in adolescents found that cognitive behavioral therapy (CBT) led to remission in nearly 65 percent of cases, a higher rate than either supportive therapy or family therapy.[11] CBT also resulted in a more rapid treatment response.

In this type of therapy, teens in a group are taught to identify and challenge unrealistic negative thoughts and beliefs. It is imperative to understand that teens (and adults) can be *taught* to recognize and combat negative patterns of thought, belief, and behavior. A Kaiser study published in the December 2001 issue of the *Archives of General Psychiatry* looked at a group of children who were at greater risk than the general population for depression because one or both parents were depressed. Half of the children whose parents were depressed received fifteen one-hour group CBT sessions with a trained therapist. The other half received whatever help they were or were not already getting. Over the next year, 29 percent of those in the control group became depressed, compared to 9 percent of the children who went to the group program. Interpersonal therapy focusing on developing healthier relationships can also be helpful.[12]

TAKE-AWAY MESSAGE

Teen depression lasting more than a week or so is not normal and should be evaluated by a health professional. Nutrition, exercise, stress relief, and instruction in coping with life's ups and downs can prevent or relieve depression.

SUPPLEMENTS FOR EMOTIONAL STABILITY AND DEPRESSION

The following supplements can help to stabilize brain chemicals to improve mood and feelings of well-being. The ultimate goal is to improve the everyday diet so that food alone provides the balance.

- L-glutamine—500 mg taken 2 to 3 times per day: Relieves sugar and starch cravings and aids relaxation.
- GABA—100-500 mg taken 2 to 3 times per day: An excellent natural way to improve calmness and muscle relaxation, and to reduce anxiety.
- L-tyrosine—500 mg taken 2 to 3 times daily: Amino acid for improving focus, mental energy, and concentration.
- 5-HTP—50 mg taken either at bedtime or, if necessary, 2 to 3 times per day: Helps with sleep, relief of depression, and nighttime cravings. One of my favorites.

- □ L-tryptophan taken either in the evening or at bedtime: By prescription as a sleep aid or for depression or pain relief.
- □ B vitamins (combination or complex) taken daily: Necessary for the brain chemical production.
- □ Zinc taken daily: Ensures adequate brain chemicals to feel balanced. Amino acids will not work adequately without appropriate zinc and B-vitamin levels.
- □ St. John's Wort taken in a 300 mg dose (0.3% hypericin) 1 to 3 times daily: Increases serotonin levels and should not be used with prescription antidepressants. May be combined with 5-HTP for better action only if necessary.[13]

WHAT YOU NEED TO KNOW
ABOUT USING AMINO ACID SUPPLEMENTS

1. Take them about twenty minutes before a meal or at least ninety minutes after. Do not take with a meal.
2. Do not take them with protein. (They will compete for absorption.)
3. L-tyrosine, tryptophan, and 5-HTP compete for absorption, so take them at different times.
4. Take the amino acids for a short time while improving the diet, which is frequently an underlying cause of problem, and increasing the amount of sleep to eight to nine hours a night. Then begin tapering off.
5. Side effects can include headaches, tiredness, and jitteriness. If side effects occur, consult your medical provider.
6. Consider using a multi–amino acid supplement long-term if you are having a difficult time managing your diet or have ongoing stress.

FOODS THAT ARE ESPECIALLY HIGH IN TRYPTOPHAN

turkey	shrimp
pork	chicken
beef	tofu
seeds (sesame, pumpkin,	kelp
and sunflower)	bananas
wild game	milk

WHAT MOMS CAN DO TODAY

1. Keep the lines of communication open. Just because she says she doesn't want to talk doesn't mean you shouldn't keep trying.
2. Call a mental health professional for advice if her "blues" last more than a few weeks.
3. If she mentions suicide, believe her. Call a mental health professional for an appointment immediately.
4. Be sure she eats a balanced diet with adequate protein.
5. If a doctor suggests antidepressants, ask about testing for hormone and amino acid levels first.
6. Realize that complex problems usually require significant time and energy to correct; quick fixes may not have long-term positive results.
7. Promote family activities to keep your teen connected.
8. Help your daughter set priorities to reduce stress.

9. Request hormone testing. Low progesterone can lead to depression. High testosterone can be associated with irritability, rage, and aggression. Additionally, low ferritin or iron levels can contribute to low moods.

10. Trust your maternal instincts.

5

STOPPING THE FAT TRAIN—
THE INSULIN LOCOMOTIVE

If you don't know that U.S. teens are getting heavier, you haven't been to the mall lately. Some girls attempt to conceal their bulk with baggy clothing, but a surprising number flaunt their excess pounds with tight jeans and skimpy tops, baring their protruding bellies. So many teens are overweight that, despite the national dieting mania and an obsession with thinness, a comfort level with obesity has developed. Not surprisingly, clothing manufacturers have jumped in with new lines catering to over-weight teens. *But look, Mom! Everybody's doing it!* When most of their friends are too heavy, family members are overweight, and every other kid in school is packing flab, being pudgy is one more way for a teen to fit in.

Statistics support the notion that being overweight is becoming the norm rather than the exception. US teens have higher rates of obesity than those in fourteen other industrialized countries, according to a 2004 Danish study, which showed that among US fifteen-year-old girls, 15 percent were obese and 31 percent were more modestly overweight.[1] If my arithmetic is correct, that means that 46 percent of teen girls are too heavy. They certainly don't lack for role models. An astounding 61 per-cent to 65 percent of American adults is overweight or obese.

THE STEEP PRICE OF OBESITY

Overweight teens are developing health problems that were once rarely seen in anyone under age twenty. What was known twenty-five years ago as adult onset diabetes is now called type 2 diabetes. A full-blown epidemic in the adult population, diabetes is an emerging epidemic among teens and children. The Centers for Disease Control and Prevention warned in 2003 that one in every three US children born in 2000 will become diabetic unless many more people start eating less and exercising more.[2] Two decades ago only 2 percent of new cases of what was then called adult onset diabetes was diagnosed in children ages nine to nineteen. Today nearly 20 percent of those with the diagnosis are in that age group. Why? Genetic predisposition may have something to do with it, but primarily it is the deadly duo—overweight and inactivity.

In addition to the real and immediate threat of developing insulin resistance, a precursor to type 2 diabetes, and other indications of metabolic syndrome (see below), being overweight puts a teen at greater lifetime risk for heart disease, cancer, bone fractures and osteoporosis, polycystic ovary syndrome (PCOS), and respiratory diseases. The psychological consequences of obesity—emotional pain, depression, and low self-esteem—can mark her for a lifetime.

WHAT IS A HEALTHY WEIGHT?

The most accurate tool doctors have for determining whether a teen's weight is appropriate for her height is called the body mass index (BMI). It has largely replaced the height and weight charts of the past, although some pediatricians still use the charts to monitor development. For children and teens, a BMI-for-age calculator is used. You can access the Mayo Clinic BMI calculator for kids at: www.mayoclinic.com/health/bmi calculator/CC00043.

The BMI involves using a fancy calculation to come up with a number that indicates underweight, normal weight, overweight, or obesity, but the online calculators make it easy. The Mayo Clinic site tells you what your child's BMI is, whether it indicates normal or overweight, and what the healthy range is for a girl her age and height. As the site points out, a healthy BMI is a moving target for growing children. Kids obviously get taller and heavier as they mature, but the relationship between weight and height varies depending on age and sex. The chart below lets you plot where your child is in relationship to other girls her age.

If your daughter is older than sixteen and she sure *looks* like an adult, you may also want to consult an adult BMI chart. To determine BMI, go to the National Institutes of Health online BMI calculator, http://nhlbisupport.com/bmi/. You may be surprised, but it doesn't take many extra pounds to be considered too heavy. For example, a 5´5´ person weighing 150 pounds has a BMI of 25 and is considered overweight. If she weighs 180 pounds and her BMI is 30, she is officially obese.

METABOLIC SYNDROME—THE DANGER ZONE

Metabolic syndrome is a sinister collection of disorders including several of the following:

- □ High blood pressure (130+ diastolic, 85+ systolic)
- □ High triglycerides (a type of fat in the blood, +150)
- □ Abnormal cholesterol, HDL (high density lipoprotein<50)
- □ Obesity, especially around the middle (35+-inch waist)
- □ Fasting blood sugar +110

The syndrome has become common among teens—and even some preteens—who are overweight and physically inactive. Their diets might go something like this: Pop-Tarts and juice or sugary cereal for breakfast, if breakfast is even eaten, and pizza and soda for lunch; candy or other sugary snacks after school washed down with soda or juice; boxed macaroni and cheese with wieners for dinner, and maybe a glass of milk, but just as likely another soda or fruit juice; ice cream with cookies before bed, or maybe a root-beer float. Sound familiar?

A kid who consumes such a diet is going to balloon, guaranteed. She is also likely to be sluggish, depressed, unable to concentrate, and at risk for developing one or more of the disorders comprising the metabolic syndrome, conditions that often lead to diabetes. *The Archives of Pediatrics and Adolescent Medicine* in 2003 reported that 4 percent of, or just over one million, American overweight teens meet the criteria for metabolic syndrome.[3] The underlying condition of this syndrome is thought to be insulin resistance.

INSULIN RESISTANCE

Insulin may be the last hormone that comes to mind when the words *raging hormones* and *teen girls* are linked, but this potent hormone, produced by the pancreas to regulate blood sugar, can turn a teen's life upside down and inside out. When she is gaining weight, has flickering energy levels, and can't decide between a nap and a big bowl of chocolate ice cream, insulin resistance is likely part of the story. (To eliminate the dilemma, she will probably eat the ice cream *then* take a nap.)

Insulin is the fat-storage hormone. Refined carbohydrates, such as those in cake, ice cream, sodas—and even pasta and potatoes—are quickly converted to sugar in the blood and cause insulin to spike. When this happens a lot (several times daily for a majority of people eating the typical American diet), a flood of insulin whooshes the sugar into cells followed by a corresponding dearth of insulin and low blood sugar—the infamous hypoglycemic sugar highs and lows. Eventually, the cells get sick and tired of all that insulin and become resistant to it. Their receptor sites turn off the lights. Nobody's home. Sorry.

Muscle cells are the first to resist, and it should come as no surprise that fat cells are the last to throw in the towel. They continue to accept sugar for storage long after muscle cells are boycotting, and abdominal fat cells are especially accommodating. That is why insulin resistance is a big factor in weight gain and so many people have spare tires around their middles. If sugar surges continue unabated, eventually the heavy demands on the insulin-making cells in the pancreas cause insulin production to slow or stop. Then too much glucose remains in the blood, and insulin resistance has crossed over into type 2 diabetes.

DOES SHE HAVE INSULIN RESISTANCE?

If you suspect that your daughter's weight gain and food cravings indicate insulin resistance, ask her to take this quiz. The more "yes" answers, the more likely that insulin resistance is a problem.

1. Do you eat candy, chips, sugary breakfast cereals, or other junk food five or more times per week?
2. Does your energy hit peaks and valleys throughout the day?
3. Have you been told that you are hypoglycemic (low blood sugar) or that you have high blood pressure?
4. Is losing weight really difficult even when you exercise?
5. Is your weight concentrated around your midsection?
6. Do you like to eat "white" foods such as bread, pasta, rice, and potatoes?
7. Do you weigh more than ten pounds more than you would like to?
8. Do you crave sweets and starchy snacks?
9. Do you feel tired soon after eating?

WHAT'S SO BAD ABOUT DIABETES?

Insulin resistance is a precursor to diabetes, and it is essential to understand the gravity of this disease. It can affect the eyes, kidneys, nerves, gums, teeth, and blood vessels. It can result in blindness, amputation, kidney failure, and heart disease. It can lead to cardiac disease as early as the thirties, and it can shorten life by an average of fifteen years. These major health problems are why it is so important to nail down whether an overweight teen is moving into the danger zone of the metabolic syndrome. How can you tell whether she's flirting with peril? One strong and readily evident indicator is if she is packing excess weight around the middle. If your girl's tummy is bulging beneath her tee shirt, ask your doctor to order a fasting coronary risk blood lipid panel for her at her next checkup, which should be scheduled soon.

DIABETES PREVENTION—SOME GOOD NEWS

Since so many people, including children and teens, are walking around with type 2 diabetes, and may even be walking with a spring in their step, some people may assume that modern medical science has it under control. The truth is that type 2 diabetes is under the control *only* of the person who has it. The good news is that insulin resistance can be reversed, and type 2 diabetes can be controlled.

Big surprise! Diet and exercise are the keys. While medications are sometimes used to control type 2 diabetes, proper diet and adequate exercise are the first lines of treatment. Exercise is as important as diet because it raises the good cholesterol, high-density lipoproteins (HDL), even without weight loss. Losing 10 percent to 15 percent of body weight decreases blood pressure and increases cell sensitivity to insulin. If you suspect that your daughter is insulin resistant or headed in that direction, encouraging her to increase her activity level is the first best thing you can do. Next, tackle the diet. Chapter 6 provides guidelines and strategies.

TOUGH CASES—CARBOHYDRATE ADDICTS

Some teens have a tougher time than others in putting the brakes on refined carbohydrate consumption. These teens have been eating breadlike and sugar-saturated foods and gulping sugary sodas and juices for so long that they are addicted. Drs. Richard F. and Rachael F. Heller, the authors of *Carbohydrate-Addicted Kids*, list symptoms for carb addiction that include swings in energy, moods, and ability to concentrate; heightened emotionality; unexplained withdrawals or outbursts; and weight problems or incidents of uncontrollable eating.[4] For carb-addicted kids, attempts to control their own eating are thwarted by intense hunger and food cravings. These are the youngsters who may hide food and eat in secret, and who can't get enough of rice, pasta, potatoes, cake, pie, and ice cream. Although most carb-addicted youths are overweight, others are not. If you suspect your daughter is enslaved to carbs, the Hellers' book offers detailed steps to using food to balance insulin and blood sugar levels.

THE TOXIC AMERICAN FOOD CULTURE

So what is to blame for the plague of obesity? Few observers of the US scene would debate that processed and fast foods are at the greasy glucose-rich roots of the epidemic. Consider the guts of the average US supermarket. Fresh produce, meats, and dairy products form the perimeter, and a majority of what is in the middle have literally been through the mill. The prevailing American diet features factory food that is processed, cheap, convenient, ever available, and super-sized.

Sodas and sweetened drinks have emerged as the single largest source of calories in the American diet, and this mania is especially ironic. The United States is one of the more fortunate developed countries in which inexpensive, safe drinking water is plentiful. We even water our lawns and wash our cars with potable water, a degree of waste that would dumbfound Third World residents. They would also be incredulous to learn that although the vast majority of US residents have potable drinking water gushing from their home faucets, we spend millions every year on bottled water. Despite the abundance of fresh water, bottled or not, millions of Americans routinely pay good money to guzzle sugary sodas and so-called "fruit" juices instead. Twenty-five years ago, teens drank almost twice as much milk as soda. Today they drink twice as much soda as milk.

Teens may be hearing in health class that sodas and sugar are bad, and veggies and whole grains are good, but that information is countered by a relentless blast of ads touting gigantic burgers and fries, and it is reinforced by mile after mile of fast-food restaurants and a plethora of junk-food advertising aimed at young people. With the exception of California, which in 2005 banned junk food from public schools, most school lunch programs are a national disgrace. The food in the school cafeteria too often looks like what's for lunch at McDonald's or Pizza Hut, and campus vending machines routinely dispense what might as well be brain poison: sodas, chips, cookies, and candy. This is confusing to kids. Why would schools provide food that is harmful? (The same could be asked of the dietary departments of some hospitals.) The sad truth is that schools reflect the culture, and the culture is hooked on junk.

Just look at the average supermarket, where fresh foods form a fringe, and the store's innards are stacked with cans and packages of processed foods. Processed food is no longer as nature intended. I have no problem with vegetables and fruits that have been minimally processed by freezing, drying, or canning. I'm talking primarily about grains that have been pounded, pulverized, bleached, dyed, loaded with chemicals, pressed into uniform shapes, sealed in fancy packaging, and placed at eye level on supermarket shelves. Most cereals, crackers, cookies, and chips fit into this sorry lot. Sadly, breads, bagels, and buns made with refined grains aren't much better. Trust me. If manufacturers (since when did food have to be "manufactured"?) have to add dyes, chemicals, vitamins, and artificial flavors, there is not much left of the original food.

As if the typical grocery cart doesn't hold enough junk, a 2004 study published in the journal *Pediatrics* reported that every day nearly one-third of US children ages four to nineteen eat fast food. The findings suggest that fast-food consumption has increased fivefold among children since 1970, and it likely packs on about six extra pounds per child per year.[5] Fast-food loving kids consumed more fats, sugars, and carbohydrates, and fewer fruits and nonstarchy vegetables than kids who didn't eat fast food. In short, they got fatter and less healthy.

Lawsuits against fast-food restaurants for making people fat have not been successful. A federal judge in 2003 threw out a lawsuit alleging McDonald's food was responsible for making people obese. The judge ruled that the plaintiff failed to show that McDonald's food was "dangerous in any way other than that which was open and obvious to a reasonable consumer." Lawyers representing McDonald's said in part, "Every responsible person understands what is in products such as hamburgers and fries, as well as the consequence to one's waistline, and potentially to one's health, of excessively eating those foods over a prolonged period of time."

Well, hello. Do you see what's wrong with that statement? It is the word *responsible*. Children are not responsible for their own nutrition, and few teens who grew up on fast food, often lured in as young children by those bright, seductive playgrounds, possess the knowledge to make informed food choices. Burgers and fries taste good, and they're cheap. It isn't intuitive that these foods are unhealthy.

Moms need to step up to the plate. The courts aren't going to do it, and by the time schools turn their lunch programs around, if they ever do, it will be too late for hundreds of thousands of kids. Teens who typically eye the world with wry and youthful cynicism are as susceptible as anybody else to the US paradox of plenty—and the mixed messages they get when soda machines are placed down the hall from the health education classroom. If nothing else, they need to know the facts about the negative effects on the brain and the body of eating too many refined grains, sugars, and bad fats. Who is going to tell them?

HER LAST BEST HOPE? YOU!

If you are reading this book, you are likely ready to begin the hard work of change with your daughter, beginning with nutrition. Overnight reform rarely sticks. It is the in-it-for-the-long-haul commitment that leads to improved health and vitality. Let's face it. So-called "diets" don't work, especially with teens. For starters, imposing an eating regimen on a teen against her will is a virtual impossibility, and preachy speeches aren't going to cut it either.

I will be the first to acknowledge this is a huge challenge. Nearly every member of my family has struggled with carb cravings and expanding waistlines (including me). I know it is an uphill battle when the world seems aligned against healthy eating and junk food and its advertising is everywhere. But I am not without hope that we may be on the verge of changing attitudes. There's that ambitious junk-food ban in California public schools, a new rule in some elementary schools replacing cupcakes and pizza with classroom supplies such as pencils and markers for birthday celebrations; and Gerber, as well as numerous competitors, is now selling organic baby food. More and more grocery stores include natural food sections, and popular public figures such as Oprah are speaking out about healthy diet and exercise. All this may signal a trend toward greater nutritional awareness and healthier eating.

Some optimistic nutritionists envision a national educational campaign along the lines of the successful public-health campaign against smoking, but don't hold your breath. The food industry is a powerful economic force, and despite the official federal recognition that obesity is a national health crisis, inducing the government to adopt policies to dissuade people from eating refined and/or fast food is not in our immediate future. Your daughter is being programmed about nutrition by corporations selling junk food that is robbing people of all ages of their health and well-being. Like it or not, her reprogramming will be largely up to you.

NO OVERNIGHT WONDER—PATIENCE!

Like any fundamental change, dietary improvement takes time. It requires more thought in the grocery store, more time in the kitchen, and, if you make a commitment to organic products, more money at check out. Your daughter may resist and demand her comfort foods. Educate her. Let her know the reasons behind the changes you are making in the family diet. If you sharply reduce the amount of breads, chips, and sweets and increase protein and vegetables (see Chapter 7 for details), and she doesn't sneak too many treats on the side, she will begin to look and feel better in short order. She will notice improved concentration, more energy, increased stamina, better mood, and a shrinking waistline.

Then it will get easier. Don't give up! Deflect her insults. Accept her horrid moods and rejections. Nobody ever said that being a mother is easy. Someday she will remember your persistence and your great example, and she will love you for showing her the way when she most needed guidance.

WHAT MOMS CAN DO TODAY

1. Gross her out. Measure 40 teaspoons of sugar into a clear glass and set it next to a Big Gulp drink container. Yup. That's how much sugar you get from drinking one of those things. Four grams equals one teaspoon of sugar.
2. Gross her out again. Buy a small can of yellow Crisco. (But be sure not to eat it as Crisco is loaded with trans fat!) Measure onto a dinner plate five tablespoons of fat, the amount contained in one Big Mac with large fries. She'll never look at a burger and fries in quite the same way.
3. Encourage her to read this chapter to get a better understanding of the long-term effects of being overweight and why her spare tire, if she has one, is bad news.
4. Encourage her to read any of the books, or parts thereof, listed in Appendix A.
5. Set a sterling example of healthy eating.

6. Get the entire family on board with improving the daily diet.

7. Involve your daughter in food preparation and make it fun. Teach her about color on the plate. Try new things.

8. Eat as many meals as possible together as a family.

9. Get involved in her school to get sodas and junk food out and PE classes in.

10. If she is seriously overweight with a BMI of twenty-eight or higher, get her an appointment with a health-care practitioner, a nutritionist, a personal trainer, or another third party whose opinion she will respect and whose advice she is likely to heed.

6

EATING FOR LIFE

If ever a teen seemed hopelessly mired in the toxic American diet and the plague of overweight, it was fourteen-year-old Kimberly. A super-sized burger with fries, a giant soda, and a hot pastry dessert was her favorite meal; Oreos with chocolate milk and Doritos with Coke were her snacks of choice; and chocolate peanut butter ice cream was her bedtime ritual. At school she devoured the nutrient-deficient factory foods stocked in the vending machines. She reported being hungry all the time, and she sometimes scooped spoonfuls of brown sugar directly from the bag.

Her mother brought her to my office because—surprise, surprise—Kimberly had become supersized herself. Despite the low-fat diets that her mom had repeatedly tried to impose, she carried 175 pounds on her 5′1″ frame, giving her a BMI of 33.1. In other words, Kimberly was officially obese. She had a family history of diabetes, and the girl's mother, to her great credit, wanted to help prevent the disease in her daughter.

Kimberly had strong cravings for sweets and breads, performed poorly in school, hated physical exertion, and often felt tired and moody. Her lab tests indicated that she was insulin resistant and headed for type 2 diabetes. After spending nearly ninety minutes with me and the office nutrition and fitness coordinator, Kimberly considered these questions: *Would you like to be in better shape and feel good most of the time? Are you willing to do what it takes?*

Fortunately, her affirmative answers opened the door for a plan her mom had not been able to implement. You can lead a teen to a healthier way to live, but you can't make her accept it. An outside authority, such as a family health practitioner, nutrition counselor, health club advisor, or other knowledgeable third party, can be the catalyst for the lifestyle transformation that girls like Kimberly need. Moms may be the single most important influence on their teens, but sometimes they need a little help from their "friends."

Kimberly left the office with a strategy for a lifestyle turnaround, the principles of which will be described in this chapter. She was not sentenced to a deprivation diet or subjected to a rigorous gym routine. Instead, she was provided a map with clear directions toward a healthier life. It was doable!

Kimberly eased into the program during the ensuing months, and her mother reported that the entire family committed to join her, a fact that was absolutely crucial to her success. A year later, Kimberly, now fifteen and an inch taller, had a healthy BMI of just under 24. Buoyed by her success and hooked on looking and feeling good, she had grasped how to manage on her own and had come to enjoy healthy eating and the fun she derived from an energetic dance class.

Kimberly had dieted before but failed to maintain weight loss. Why? Because like just about any female who has tried to lose weight in the past thirty years, she was sentenced to a low-fat, low-calorie diet, dooming her to failure. The word *diet* has come to mean something you submit to for weight loss, then abandon to return to whatever you were eating before. With her new plan-for-life, Kimberly was finally off the diet seesaw. Sadly, legions of teens do not share her good fortune.

A WEIGHTY ISSUE—LOSING POUNDS AND KEEPING THEM OFF

Is there a US teen who has not obsessed about weight or a female past age thirteen who has not been on a diet? I think not. Girls begin comparing themselves to stick-figure models as early as age seven or eight, and boy, do they come up fat, even when they aren't. Our culture is weight obsessed and diet addicted. Yet we are the fattest nation in the world! About half the population really needs to lose weight, and there is no shortage of authors writing books about how to do it.

I am not pretending to offer anything revolutionary, but what I have to say is tried and true. If your daughter, or anyone else in the family, is struggling with weight, listen up. This chapter provides dietary principles and guidelines that will produce energy, well-being, and healthy weight for a lifetime. The principles are simple:

1. Eat protein.
2. Eat good fats.
3. Be picky about carbohydrates.
4. Get rid of sugar and refined grains.
5. Eat whole grains, preferably organic and unprocessed.
6. Eat your fruits and veggies.
7. Keep metabolism stoked by eating at least three meals a day starting with a good breakfast.
8. Exercise daily.

If your daughter is into the typical American fare heavy on breads and sweets and processed and fast foods, moving into a healthier realm may be a challenge. Can she learn to prefer broccoli with butter to ketchup and fries? A sliced apple with cheddar to cake and ice cream? Green salad and olive oil dressing to macaroni and cheese? I hope so, because that's what it comes down to—choosing foods that taste great and are good for her now and forever over foods that will eventually make her fat, fatigued, and sad. Getting started is a matter of recognizing that food really *is* the most powerful drug we put into our bodies every day, then taking that first step.

HOW TO EAT WELL ON A BUDGET

Organic, natural, and whole foods are generally more expensive than the mass-produced, nutrient-deficient, chemical-laden packaged factory foods so typical today. You will probably end up spending more if you buy whole organic products, but you don't have to bust the budget to make them part of your family's healthy diet. Some suggestions for making the most of your food dollar:

☐ Buy bulk. Many markets have bins of grains, pastas, dried fruits, nuts, cereals, flours, spices, teas, legumes, and more from which you scoop out as much as you want into a plastic bag, write the bin number on a twist tie, and weigh it at the checkout. Molasses, honey, and extra-virgin olive oil can also be purchased in bulk, and many stores have a grind-your-own-nut-butters area. You save a lot by buying in bulk, because you are not paying for packaging or product advertising.

☐ Eat in season. Stock up on fruits and veggies in season and freeze them. Blueberries, one of the richest sources of anti-oxidants, are easily frozen on a cookie sheet, then rolled into freezer bags to enjoy all winter. Farmers' markets are great places to load up on summer veggies when they are abundant, relatively inexpensive, and at their nutritional peak.

☐ Join your local food co-op. If you live in a city or a college town, there is probably one nearby. For a membership fee, you can get a discount on the whole, natural foods that co-ops typically stock, and if you can volunteer a few hours a month, the discount is even greater. Check out this Web site to find the co-op in your neighborhood: www.coopdirectory.org.

☐ Watch for coupons and sales. Many natural products have coupons to be redeemed at the checkout. If you have favorite products, check their Web sites for specials and incentives.

AN EIGHT-STEP GUIDE

Here is an eight-step guide to healthier eating and achieving normal weight.

1. Eat protein. Protein is your daughter's friend. Eggs, meats, fish, dairy products, certain combinations of whole grains, and some soy products all provide the brain and muscle fuel she needs. Without protein, we lose muscle mass, slow our metabolism, and gain weight. Insufficient protein leads to physical and emotional fatigue. It is good to eat protein with each meal.

2. Eat good fat. We have been fed a big fat lie about fat for so long that it seems heretical to dispute it. It is, however, being effectively disputed in science-based books and journals. This is a topic too complex to be discussed thoroughly here, but several excellent resources are listed under "Recommended Reading" in Appendix A. The upshot: it is right and good to eat fat, including extra-virgin olive, sesame, and flax oils, and the saturated fats in butter, eggs, meats, and unrefined coconut oil. They will not clog your arteries and send you straight to the grave as we have been led to believe. Research scientists, such as nutritionist Mary Enig, PhD, are demonstrating that saturated fats play important beneficial roles in body chemistry and actually help to prevent rather than cause heart disease. In the 2005 book *Eat Fat, Lose Fat*, Enig and coauthor Sally Fallon lay out the scientific evidence for eating a traditional diet high in saturated fats. I realize this goes against everything you have read or heard for decades, but Enig and Fallon present compelling arguments, as do the authors of the studies they cite and the authors of other books and articles listed as resources.[1]

We need fat from the very beginning. Breast-fed babies start life on a high-fat diet; mother's milk is nearly 50 percent fat, most of it saturated, and provides one of the highest proportions of cholesterol of nearly any food. Fats are concentrated energy for the body and building blocks for cells and hormones. They improve our hair and skin and contribute to our feeling of being satisfied after a meal. They slow metabolism and nutrient absorption so that we can go longer before food cravings or hunger strikes. Fat-soluble vitamins, such as A, E, D, and K, need fat to carry them to cells.

But before we go whole hog, remember that there are good fats and bad fats. Fats we should avoid are *partially hydrogenated oils*, which contain trans fatty acids (or trans fats). They are present in chips, French fries, most commercial baked goods, most pizza crusts, and most restaurant meals that include fried or baked foods. Even breakfast cereals contain them, especially those that promise to deliver "crunch." These fats have been altered to give processed foods a shelf life longer than Methuselah's. Trans fats contribute to heart disease, type 2 diabetes, and arterial inflammation. Trans fats have no redeeming qualities, other than enabling the mega food industry to cut its spoilage losses at our peril. If you see "partially hydrogenated" in a product's ingredient list, drop the product and run screaming down the aisle. Congratulate yourself while making a spirited rush toward the natural foods and produce sections of the market, where whole and unrefined foods are bursting with nutrients.

The bottom line for fats: include good fat as at least 30 percent to 40 percent of daily calories. In real terms, even if weight loss is the goal, that means it is okay to drizzle olive oil or use a pat of butter on cooked veggies, drink a glass of whole milk, and eat a steak about the size of your palm. Fat creates a feeling of fullness and provides a slow burn that prevents food cravings. And, as Enig and Fallon point out, saturated fat (they highly recommend coconut oil) is best if weight loss is desired.[2]

3. Be selective about carbohydrates. Know the glycemic index (GI). The GI ranks carbohydrates according to how long it takes the body to convert them into blood sugar. The longer it takes, the better. Foods high on the index, such as refined flour, white rice, and sugar convert almost instantly and produce a sharp rise in insulin production and blood glucose levels. (Insulin is the fat-storage hormone, remember?) Insulin surges cause blood sugar to spike then plummet, creating cravings for more carbohydrates and hence weight gain, while a slow burn suppresses hunger and leads to weight loss. Foods low on the index, such as lentils and many vegetables, create a slow burn and more stable insulin production.

Carbohydrates, but not all of them and only in limited quantities, are good for growing girls, especially for teens who need to lose weight. Controlled carbohydrate diets work. If your daughter is trying to achieve a healthy weight, she should keep her carbohydrate consumption in the 70- to 120-grams-a-day range and stay low on the GI. The first things out the window in my recommended weight-loss plan are sugar and anything made with refined (white) grains, all of which are carbohydrate-heavy, super high on the GI, and take up about half the space in the typical grocery store. Unprocessed meats and fats don't contain carbohydrates, but all fruits, vegetables, legumes, and grains do, and that is why it is important to learn to use the GI. But there is more to it than weight control. In 1999 the World Health Organization recommended that people in industrialized countries base their diets on low-GI foods to prevent coronary heart disease and type 2 diabetes, as well as obesity; and studies from the Harvard School of Public Health indicate that type 2 diabetes and heart disease are strongly related to the GI of the overall diet.[3]

The take-away message: become familiar with the GI, avoid the foods that are high on the list, and include foods low on the list. For a complete guide to the GI, see www.glycemicindex.com. This site from the University of Sydney is an extensive, authoritative source for classifying foods from around the world.

EXAMPLES OF CARBOHYDRATES RATED HIGH OR LOW ON THE GLYCEMIC INDEX

High-glycemic	Lower-glycemic
potatoes (sorry, hold the fries!)	most legumes—beans, lentils
white rice	whole fruits, especially berries
bananas	—not fruit juices
white bread	whole grains—wheat, oats,
white pasta	barley
refined breakfast cereals	brown rice
soft drinks	bulgur
fruit juices	whole grain breakfast cereals
sugar, honey, corn syrup	—no sugar added
	ccouscous

4. Get sugar and refined grains out of her life! Refined sugar is a chemical product derived from sugar cane or sugar beets, from which every nutrient has been stripped. Refined sugar has zero food value and is a complete waste of calories. It is present in most manufactured foods and hides in products where you wouldn't expect to find it, such as in deli meats and canned soups. It is difficult to get away from it, but the point is to build sugar awareness and avoid it as much as possible. Start by scrutinizing labels. A teaspoon of sugar weighs about 4 grams. If a label says a food contains 12 grams, that equals about 3 teaspoons of sugar. Sugar goes by several names, including sucrose, dextrose, lactose, maltose, maltodextrin, brown sugar, raw sugar, fructose, corn syrup, high-fructose corn syrup, and white grape juice.

What about sugar substitutes? Some artificial sweeteners, such as saccharin, acesulfame-K, and aspartame (NutraSweet), should be avoided. All are widely used and hide in the unlikeliest places. (Check out the ingredients in your toothpaste, for example.) NutraSweet is used in many diet sodas and in numerous commercial baked goods, chewing gum, gelatin desserts, and dietetic products. The Center for Science in the Public Interest (CSPI) warns that these sweeteners are unsafe and/or untested and not worth the risk.[4]

The sugar substitutes I recommend include stevia, agave, and xylitol. All are derived from plants and safely satisfy a sweet tooth. These sweeteners are available at most grocery stores. All should be used in moderation, however, because encouraging a sweet tooth can be self-defeating, especially if weight is an issue.

Soda is the sugar-delivery system of choice in the United States. I don't know how sodas came to be known as "soft" drinks, because there are a lot of hard facts about them. American teens now drink twice as much soda as milk, a reverse of figures noted twenty years ago, according to the CSPI's report, *Liquid Candy*. It says that the average soda consumption among girls between ages thirteen and eighteen who drink soda is two cans a day, and 10 percent drink more than five cans a day.[5] A girl who drinks five cans of soda a day consumes an incredible 700 absolutely worthless calories and more than 68 teaspoons of sugar! Just one soda averages 140 calories and 39 grams of sugar, which translates into nearly 10 teaspoons of sugar.

THIS IS FOOD?

Can you identify this food from the ingredient list?

Corn syrup, enriched flour (niacin, iron, thiamine mononitrate, riboflavin, sugar, water, partially hydrogenated vegetable and/or animal shortening (contains one or more of: canola oil, corn oil, cottonseed oil, soybean oil) eggs, skim milk; contains 2 percent or less of: whey, modified food starch, salt, leavening (baking soda, monocalcium phosphate, sodium acid pyrophosphate) mono- and diglycerides, lecithin, sodium stearoyl lactylate, and artificial flavors, artificial colors (red 40 and yellow 5), sorbic acid (to retard spoilage). Answer: Hostess Twinkies.

5. Eat whole grains and/or sprouted grains, preferably organically grown. There's a lot of confusion about what constitutes a whole grain. Here's the deal. A whole grain is one that comes in its original "packaging" with nothing added, nothing removed. It may be in whole kernel form, such as rice, or pressed flat like old-fashioned oats. It contains the live germ and, if planted, could sprout. Processed grains are flat-out dead, and the germ, exposed to oxygen because its protective covering, the bran, has been removed, can become rancid. Many so-called whole-wheat products list enriched flour as the first ingredient and include food coloring or molasses to add a brownish tint. Any flour that is enriched has first had its life force ripped out through a refining process.

As for breads, sprouted grain products are best because they contain the whole grain, and presoaking makes them easier to digest and increases the vitamin content. The Alvardo Street Bakery, Food for Life, and the Silver Hills Bakery are among the many companies that sprout whole live grains to make bread products that are virtually flourless. Sprouting releases stored vitamins and minerals. These flavorful products retain the grain's natural fiber and bran. Sprouted grain products can be found in refrigerated or frozen food areas of many supermarkets, or in health food sections. They cost more, but isn't good health worth it? Food for Life quotes the Bible on its package of 100 percent flourless, sprouted whole-grain cinnamon raisin English muffins. "Take also unto thee Wheat and Barley and Beans and Lentils and Millet and Spelt and put them in one vessel and make bread of it" (Ezekiel 4:9). Indeed, the muffins include all those grains. Whole, unprocessed nutrient-dense grains supply higher-quality fuel to run the body's metabolic engine. Grains are complex carbohydrates, and they have a place in the diet, but teens who need to lose weight should limit their consumption.

6. Eat your veggies. By now just about everybody has heard the message to include at least five servings of vegetables and fruits in the daily diet, and seven or eight are better. While a baked potato with the skin is nutritious, potatoes are high on the GI and to be avoided by teens who want to lose excess body fat. When choosing fruits and veggies, go for rich, deep color. Sweet red bell peppers, blueberries, raspberries, kale, spinach, carrots, and broccoli are among the many good choices. As for pale, watery iceberg lettuce—why bother?

7. Keep metabolism stoked. Eat at least three meals a day, and modest midmorning and midafternoon snacks help to keep the engine purring. Skipping meals and severely restricting calories is counterproductive because of how metabolism works. For the engine to run hot, it needs to be stoked. Deprived of adequate fuel, the body goes into *conservation-of-energy* mode. That's one reason that low-calorie/low-fat dieting is unnatural, unpleasant, and, most often, ineffective. Few people can realistically live in diet mode forever. They are always hungry, depriving themselves of the true pleasures of healthy eating. Then when they do go back to their usual fare, their metabolic rate has been slowed and they gain back the pounds they lost and then some.

8. Exercise! Every body needs it, and the greater the frequency, the better. It is integral to lifelong weight control and general well-being. Teens should shoot for at least a half hour of physical activity most days, and preferably one hour. Walking, running, swimming, biking, dancing, whatever works to get the heart rate elevated. Aerobic exercise boosts mood, burns calories, increases endurance, creates energy, and, in time, becomes a positive addiction, the type that helps rather than harms.

Strength-training with weights, isometric exercise, yoga, karate, and other disciplines are also highly recommended. Strength training builds muscles, and muscles burn fat. Pretty simple. Even if she does nothing else, your daughter's health and wellness will improve with regular exercise, and that is a money-back guarantee.

VEGETARIAN AND VEGAN DIETS

Too often I see girls who jump into a fad without recognizing the extra lengths they must go to eat a diet that meets their nutritional needs. Anecdotal evidence suggests that vegetarianism is fairly widespread, especially among young women, and many college cafeterias and even some high schools include vegetarian and vegan choices.

Swayed by animal rights arguments or influential peers, too many teens take on a meatless eating plan *without* a plan. They don't realize the thinking and preparation that go into a major dietary shift and shortchange themselves in some important areas. She may end up way heavy on carbohydrates and lacking in the iron, amino acids, B vitamins, and other nutrients necessary to feel good and have mental clarity. On a carb-heavy, protein-deficient diet, she can feel tired, moody, and hungry all the time, and she can even gain weight! Vegetarianism among teen girls can also signal a harmful dieting mentality that includes eating disorders. To girls with eating disorders, however, it is likely that vegetarianism is just another way to restrict calories rather than the cause of the problem.

On the positive side, some studies have shown that teen vegetarians get more dietary fiber, eat more fruits and vegetables, and consume fewer sweets and salty snack foods than do their meat-eating friends. I know many healthy, happy vegetarians who take great care with their diets. They have chosen a vegetarian lifestyle out of health concerns, care for the environment, or empathy for animals. They are educated about vegetarian nutrition and are committed to getting adequate protein and not just filling up on bread, pasta, and sweets. Teen girls who decide against meat need to recognize their ongoing need for protein, iron, zinc, calcium, vitamin B_{12}, D, and A, and riboflavin, and plan where and how they are going to get these nutrients. Vegetarians should use a supplement containing vitamin B_{12} and, if sunlight exposure is limited and dairy products are not eaten, vitamin D as well.

A WORD ABOUT THE VEGAN DIET

Adopting a vegan diet is an extreme lifestyle choice. Vegans eat no animal products whatsoever, including eggs, dairy, or any product that contains so much as a whiff of fish, fowl, or livestock. Theirs is wholly plant-based. In the adult population, vegans represent about 1 percent of all vegetarians, who account for just 2.5 percent of the overall population. The number of teen vegans is unknown, but we're not talking huge numbers. Being a vegan is a deeper level of vegetarianism and often involves a philosophical and political choice that demands nutritional education and a lot of heavy-duty planning. Vegans must work hard to get enough calories and proper nutrients. If your daughter chooses this path, it is likely she is aware that she needs to pay special attention to getting what she needs from plant foods. Buy her a good book on vegan nutrition and help her by purchasing appropriate foods.

KNOW THE NO-NOS

☐ Trans fats. These hide in nearly all processed foods, movie popcorn, margarines, and many cereals.
☐ Sugar. Read labels. Anything ending in *-ose* is a sugar. High-fructose corn syrup is a widely used sweetener in processed food.
☐ White flour and any other highly refined grain.
☐ Soda. It is nothing but sugar water.

□ Juice. Okay, have a little fresh orange juice, but remember that most juice products contain precious amounts of real fruit juice and, like soda, are mostly sugar water.

□ Processed snack foods: crackers, chips, cakes, cookies.

HOW TO FEED YOUR TEEN

Start with *breakfast*, a great big hearty, happy, healthy meal. Even teens who need to lose weight need to eat a big breakfast. Kids who skip this meal or grab a Pop-Tart on the way out the door are setting themselves up for a midmorning crash. A health-giving diet starts with breakfast. Consider it the most important meal of the day. Trash the sugary cereals, the toast and jam, the muffins, and the buttermilk pancakes and syrup, and think *protein* and good fats, brain and muscle food that will carry her through the day. While sugary cereals will precipitate a blood sugar crash about two hours after eating and lead to brain fuzz, exhaustion, and hunger, a good breakfast will fuel your daughter for hours. Studies have shown that people who eat a big breakfast eat less throughout the day and lose weight over time. Give it a try.

BREAKFAST

Combine two or more of the suggestions below for a meal to last through the morning.

1. Eggs! Eat them hard- or soft-boiled, poached, in omelets, scrambled, or fried. Two or three for breakfast are good, and don't worry about eating them several times a week. Eggs are among nature's most complete, easiest to prepare, and most economical foods. Eggs got a bad rap for years because they are rich in cholesterol and saturated fat, but here is what the authors of *Life Without Bread* have to say about eggs: "Out of the 13 vitamins, six are supplied in reasonable quantities in eggs alone. Thus consumption of eggs daily would supply at least half the body's vitamin needs, along with important fats and protein. Eggs do not represent a hazard to your health. They are arguably the most nutritious food available and also among the least costly."[6]

2. Fruit. Half a grapefruit or an orange, small banana, a half cup of berries or cantaloupe. Skip the juice.

3. Sprouted grain bread. Spread with cream cheese, nut butter, or melted cheese. Whole grain tortillas are a healthy choice too.

4. Cheese. An ounce or two of good cheese can top an omelet or be eaten plain with fruit.

5. Meat. Nitrate-free bacon or sausage, leftover meat from dinner, a slice of ham or turkey, or soy "meat" breakfast products.

6. Toast or tortillas. Stick to high-fiber, high-protein, sprouted-grain breads, tortillas, English muffins, and bagels. Top with nut butters, cream cheese, or sugar-free fruit spread.

7. High-fiber, whole-grain cereal. Old-fashioned oatmeal is best. Soak it the night before, or cook it slowly and add a tablespoon of butter or coconut oil to boost staying power. Sprinkle with ground flaxseed meal (it has a delicious nutty flavor) or ground-up almonds and a little cinnamon, then top with half-and-half, whole milk, or yogurt. Adding berries provides flavor and antioxidants. Sweeten with a bit of honey or good sugar substitute.

8. Protein bars or shakes. These are a last resort, reserved for mornings when your daughter is running late and neither of you has time to cook and eat something better.

9. Veggies. Tomato slices topped with melted cheese; leftover veggies in an omelet.

SNACKS

1. Small handful of dried fruit and nuts. (Skip the dried fruit if weight is an issue.)
2. Small apple with peanut butter or cheese.
3. Orange with one ounce of cheese.
4. Banana or celery with peanut butter.
5. One-half cup high-fiber cereal with milk.
6. Turkey or ham sandwich on one slice of sprouted grain bread, topped with lettuce leaf.
7. Chopped tomatoes, cucumbers, and chickpeas with extra-virgin olive oil and balsamic vinegar.
8. A boiled egg with one slice of sprouted grain bread.
9. One small container of plain yogurt mixed with fresh or frozen berries. Sweeten with agave, stevia, or xylitol.
10. Water-packed tuna, drained and mixed with mayo to moisten, on Wasa crackers.
11. One-half cup of cottage cheese with pineapple or other fruit.
12. Ham slices spread with cream cheese and rolled up.
13. Portion of a protein bar (less than 10 gs sugar).
14. Portion of a protein shake (less than 10 gs sugar).
15. Whole grain crackers (4–5) with peanut butter or real (not processed) cheese.

LUNCH

1. Chef salad, Wasa crackers, and a small piece of fruit.
2. Tuna, turkey, or chicken salad on a bed of greens with a small piece of fruit and two Wasa crackers. Drizzle salad with extra-virgin olive oil and vinegar.
3. Hearty veggie lentil soup with one slice of sprouted grain bread or three Wasa crackers.
4. Open-faced turkey, chicken, or ham sandwich made with sprouted grain bread. Use a romaine lettuce leaf as the top of the sandwich.
5. Protein bar or shake if there is no time to sit down to eat.

DINNER

1. Grilled chicken, salad, and small potato or a vegetable. Skip the potato and add another veggie if weight is an issue.
2. Baked or grilled fish with one-half cup brown rice and heaping cup of veggies. Drizzle with olive oil and lemon and season to taste.
3. Beef stew with barley and veggies.
4. Turkey chili with a green salad and corn bread. If weight loss is desired, skip the corn bread and double up on salad.
5. Meat or vegetarian lasagna. Discard half the noodles and substitute zucchini slices. If weight loss is desired, substitute zucchini slices for all the noodles.
6. High-protein, low-carb pasta with chicken and marinara sauce. Add broccoli and cauliflower florets and bake. Green salad.
7. Any Italian dinner without the pasta, or only one-half cup of pasta.
8. Whole-grain, low-carb tortillas with grilled chicken and veggies.
9. Baked ham with two veggies and a green salad.
10. Soup, salad, and one slice of whole grain bread.

SUPPLEMENTS TO HELP WITH WEIGHT LOSS

□ If calcium-rich foods, such as milk, yogurt, and cheese, are not eaten daily, take a calcium-magnesium supplement.

□ Consider chromium picolinate (a mineral) for blood sugar stabilization and improving insulin sensitivity. 400–600 mcg per day in divided doses before meals.

□ Consider L-glutamine (amino acids) to help control cravings, 500 mg twice daily on empty stomach.

□ If at high risk for diabetes, consider testing for insulin resistance. The tests most often ordered are fasting insulin, fasting glucose, or glucose intolerance.

WHAT MOMS CAN DO TODAY

1. Realize that change is a process and won't happen overnight. Introduce new ideas one at a time. Perhaps begin by introducing sprouted grain bread rather than serving your regular breads. Quietly quit stocking the pantry with chips and cookies, and instead load the refrigerator with fruits and veggies, preferably ready to eat with savory dips. Buy good cheese, olives, and nuts for snacks.

2. Pack her lunch if at all possible. Spare her the cafeteria or fast food!

3. Take extra time (you can do this!) to find out what she likes. Experiment. Maybe she can handle peanut butter on celery instead of crackers or ham-pickle-cream cheese roll-ups (with cute toothpicks) instead of chips.

4. Tackle one small area at a time. Start with breakfast, then revamp dinners, then stop buying junk food—get it out of the house.

5. Prepare a large bag of cut-up veggies once a week to make available for snacking. Make a healthy dip, or buy prepared humus or tofu dips.

6. Never scold over food.

7. Point out the positive aspects of whole foods, such as how this or that food will boost energy and help the brain function well.

8. Find healthy treat recipes and provide cookies or other treats occasionally to prove that you are still a real mom and not a food drill sergeant.

9. Make home-cooked meals. Try to control the number of fast-food encounters. Start using a Crock-Pot and get the food cooking during the day to avoid "desperation eating" before dinner is ready.

10. Have several of your daughter's girlfriends over and teach them what you know about insulin, fat, the brain, mood, and energy. Challenge them to a contest on eating better! Celebrate at the end with a big party with plenty of great-tasting healthy food. Invite more girls next time!

11. Pay your daughter not to eat junk—bribes work!

12. Pick your battles. Maybe you will only be able to control breakfast and dinner. Do what you can.

13. Use protein or nutrition bars that are low in sugar and have at least 14 grams of protein. Try protein smoothies, shakes, or other blends for a quick breakfast or snack.

14. Have meals as a family as often as possible.

15. If your daughter needs to lose weight and you could stand to lose a few pounds, try teamwork! Shop and cook together.

16. If applicable, ask her to read Kimberly's story at the beginning of this chapter. Let her know it could be *her* success story!

7

EATING DISORDERS

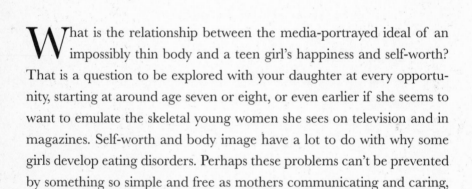

What is the relationship between the media-portrayed ideal of an impossibly thin body and a teen girl's happiness and self-worth? That is a question to be explored with your daughter at every opportunity, starting at around age seven or eight, or even earlier if she seems to want to emulate the skeletal young women she sees on television and in magazines. Self-worth and body image have a lot to do with why some girls develop eating disorders. Perhaps these problems can't be prevented by something so simple and free as mothers communicating and caring, but it's worth a shot.

Your daughter needs to know from day one that she doesn't need to look like a model to be loved and that healthy food is her friend. She also needs to be encouraged in intellectual, social, artistic, and athletic endeavors—anything to solidify her self-esteem before she hits adolescence and the torture that middle school can be for so many girls.

Can eating disorders be prevented? Some experts in the eating disorder/brain chemistry fields say that stressed-out girls who eat a high-sugar, protein-poor diet have a higher incidence of depression, anxiety, and abusive behaviors, including eating disorders. But the exact causes of eating disorders are still a mystery. It is difficult to say that if you do this or that your daughter won't develop an eating disorder, or if she already has one, she will become a well-adjusted teen delighted with her body. It is far more complicated than a step-by-step to-do list, especially after the fact. However, I believe that you can make a difference in how your daughter views her own body—and what she puts into it. (See What Moms Can Do Today at the end of this chapter.)

Eating disorders cause a lot of misery, not just to the sufferer but also to the people who love her and feel helpless to stop her self-destruction. Each month in my office, I see young women who are obsessive about food, but rather than eating too much, they eat too little, or they binge and purge. Most of the time, the teen vehemently denies having a problem, insisting that she is simply health conscious. Sometimes, however, the disorder is impossible to deny. Such was the case with sixteen-year-old Celia.

CELIA'S STORY

At 5′8″ Celia weighed just under 100 pounds. Some days she was lucky to eat 500 calories, even though most active teen girls require around 2,500 calories a day to maintain a healthy weight. Food was the enemy. She avoided fat like poison and refused to eat eggs or meat, the high-protein foods that could have prevented her from developing malnutrition. Although Celia's cheeks were sunken, her ribs were ridges beneath the taut skin of her chest, and her stomach formed a deep bowl between her sharp hipbones, she insisted she was too heavy. Her face was drawn, and dark circles under her eyes smudged her appearance. She hadn't menstruated in months. Even though she wasn't eating enough to sustain activity, she exercised obsessively, two to three hours a day *after* her school athletic practice. Her mother brought her to my office frantic with worry. She had suspected for months that something was wrong, but now Celia wanted to take a weeklong trip with her school. Was it safe for her to travel?

Well, no. It wasn't safe for her to do anything except carefully regain pounds to achieve a healthy weight, which, in Celia's case, was at least

120 to 125 pounds. The girl was literally starving. Her body was consuming muscle for fuel. While severely restricting calories and wearing herself ragged with exercise, she was depriving her body of essential nutrients during a time of physical growth, and the gynecological and hormonal effects were profound. The hormones controlling menstruation dried up, and her periods stopped. She had also developed osteopenia, bone loss that could develop into osteoporosis. What's more, starvation resulted in extremely low levels of the essential amino acids, including tryptophan, which are necessary for normal growth and development and are precursors of several substances, including serotonin and niacin. Author Julia Ross, M.A., in her book *The Diet Cure*, points out that eating disorders have their roots in the nutrient deprivation that comes with restricted calorie dieting.[1] Conversely, the compulsive bingeing and purging of bulimia and the obsessive dieting of anorexia nervosa can be reversed with amino acid supplementation and a diet with plenty of protein, good fats, vegetables, and fruit.

Celia exhibited the primary characteristics of anorexia nervosa, a severe eating disorder in which young women have a distorted body image and see themselves as fat even when they are slender or emaciated, as in Celia's case. Celia had been dieting for months, denying she had a problem. Celia was evaluated in my office for hormonal and brain chemical deficiencies and was educated on the need for amino acids. I started her on a daily amino plus liquid formulation that included all of the vitamins, minerals, amino acids, and antioxidants she needed, plus an additional twice-daily 5-HTP supplement. She was instructed to take these religiously to help with her mood disorder and to nourish and protect her body and mind from further damage. She was referred to a nutritional behaviorist who worked with her further on the eating disorder.

"ANAS" AND "MIAS"

Eating disorders are a lifestyle choice for some young women, and Internet support groups have proliferated to help them succeed. These

Web sites and discussion boards provide positive reinforcement for the skin-and-bones look and list "helpful" hints about how to avoid eating, techniques for inducing vomiting, suggestions for foods that are most easily purged, and how to conceal an eating disorder from the family. The young women (people with eating disorders are almost always teen girls or young women) who visit the sites call themselves "Anas" or "Mias" depending upon whether they are anorexic, starving themselves to the brink of cardiac arrest, or bulimic, eating small to outrageous amounts of food then throwing up. The sites include "thinspirational" photo galleries of sunken bellies, skeletal chests, and sharply defined shoulder blades, the body image goals of the so-called pro-ED (eating disorders) group. Some experts believe these sites are helping to create and perpetuate a pervasive and dangerous—to its members—subculture.

Short of locking her up, there is no practical way to keep a teen with an eating disorder from accessing Web sites that help her "keep on track" in her quest for the skeletal look. Most often, message-board visitors are looking for support, solidarity, and practical advice. Here are some typical postings, complete with message-board punctuation style:

> *Yesterday was pretty good, all I had all day at work was coffee, water, tea and gum. Then I went to the gym, and when I got home my mom MADE ME EAT! I had to do some salsa taste testing. My beautiful day ruined by four tortilla chips with salsa. Sooooo... I am trying again today:*
>
> *Coffee*
> *Water*
> *Tea*
> *Gum*
> *(And maybe a few Tums for that crappy stomach thing)*
> *Anyone want to go with me? It's lonely by myself . . .*

And another:

*i am now sitting in front of the toilet, my laptop on my knee. i've been purg-
ing for ten minutes and retching for two. That's my sign that it's all gone. i
still feel fat, so i've taken two laxies, never brave enough to take anymore. your
comments would really help.*

Occasionally some serious doubt slips in:

*sometimes i wonder why appearance has to mean this much? enough to make
you want to put your life on the line? i mean not that i would have it any other
way . . . but i feel so sick all the time, sometimes i miss the old days of just
feeling good. when each day was something to truly look forward to. now i feel
as all i have to look forward to is whether i can make it the whole day without eating, and if i don't make it i'm a failure, and if i do make it i'm so
dizzy . . . oh this life. i just want to be thin. to be thin . . . to be thin.*

But the doubt is countered by this response:

*I've been thinking about that too. And a lot of times when my stomach's
rumbling, and I can practically TASTE what other people are eating, I want
to just say 'what the hell' and go for it. But I remember what it was like, ten
years ago when I was the fat kid—and I cried myself to sleep 5 nights out
of the week. Would I go back to that? Not in a million years. So for me, anything to avoid being that girl again is worth it.*

If your gut tells you that your daughter is caught up in an eating disorder, visiting pro-ED sites can give you a glimpse straight into the minds
and hearts of young women who are deep into the lifestyle. Reading
their accounts of daily life, their hints for avoiding detection, and their
cries for support and direction might break your heart. But it may also
help you understand whether or not your daughter is in trouble, and, if
she is, provide the impetus to get her the help she needs. (See Appendix A

for where to look for help.) In the meantime, here are the basics about common eating disorders.

ANOREXIA NERVOSA

The severity of the disorder varies, and some girls may experience an episode or two then recover without professional help. Others have a pattern of weight gain and relapse, and some experience a chronic course of illness over many years, their health deteriorating steadily. It is important to seek professional help when an eating disorder is first suspected. It cannot be overemphasized that the longer the disorder is allowed to continue, the more difficult it is to overcome.

The National Institute for Mental Health reports that the annual death rate for people suffering from anorexia is about twelve times higher than the annual death rate due to all causes among females ages fifteen to twenty-four in the general population. Cardiac arrest, electrolyte imbalance, and suicide are the most common complications of the disorder.

ANOREXIA SYMPTOMS

□ Continuing weight loss, even when already thin.
□ Moodiness, sleeplessness, irritability.
□ Low self-esteem.
□ Perfectionism.
□ Obsessive exercising.
□ Tiredness and weakness.
□ Baby-like hair (lanugo) on body.
□ Thinning head hair.
□ Extreme pickiness about food.
□ Amenorrhea—absence of menstruation.

HEALTH CONSEQUENCES OF ANOREXIA

□ Abnormally slow heart rate and low blood pressure. The risk for heart failure rises as the heart rate and blood pressure sink lower and lower.

□ Reduction of bone density (osteoporosis), which usually occurs only after menopause.

□ Muscle loss and weakness.

□ Severe dehydration, which can result in kidney failure.

□ Fainting, fatigue, and overall weakness.

□ Dry hair and skin; hair loss is common.

□ Growth of a downy layer of hair called lanugo all over the body, including the face.

BULIMIA NERVOSA

Bulimia nervosa is another severe eating disorder that can have lasting consequences. The sufferer eats large amounts of food, more than would be consumed during a normal meal and often as much as 15,000 calories a day. Binges are followed immediately by secretive, self-induced vomiting. Laxatives and diuretics may also be used to purge the body. Overexercising can also be part of this syndrome. Girls suffering from this eating disorder may be of normal weight, making diagnosis more difficult.

Bulimia is not as obvious as anorexia, but is actually more common. It affects at least 3 to 10 percent of adolescent and college-age women in the United States.

BULIMIA SYMPTOMS

□ Repeated episodes of bingeing and purging, which may result in serious irritation of the esophagus.

□ Feeling out of control and disgusted with oneself during a binge, and eating beyond the point of comfortable fullness.

□ Purging after a binge, typically by self-induced vomiting, abuse of laxatives, diet pills, and/or diuretics.

□ Frequent dieting.

□ Extreme concern with body weight and shape.

□ Secretive behavior, anxiety, nervousness.

HEALTH CONSEQUENCES OF BULIMIA

- ▫ Electrolyte imbalances that can lead to irregular heartbeat and possibly heart failure and death.
- ▫ Potential for gastric (stomach) rupture during periods of bingeing.
- ▫ Inflammation and possible rupture of the esophagus from frequent vomiting.
- ▫ Tooth decay and staining from stomach acids released during frequent vomiting.
- ▫ Chronic irregular bowel movements and constipation as a result of laxative abuse.
- ▫ Peptic ulcers and pancreatitis.

COMPULSIVE OVEREATING

Binge eating, also known as compulsive overeating, is characterized by uncontrolled, impulsive, and continuous eating to the point of discomfort. Shame and self-hatred often follow the overeating episodes. Frequent attempts at dieting and fasting, anxiety, depression, and loneliness are part of this disorder. A compulsive overeater is often overweight or obese but may be of normal weight.

HEALTH CONSEQUENCES OF COMPULSIVE OVEREATING

- ▫ High blood pressure.
- ▫ High cholesterol.
- ▫ Elevated triglycerides.
- ▫ Type 2 diabetes.
- ▫ Gallbladder disease.[2]

NUMBERS AREN'T HIGH— UNLESS SHE'S YOUR TEEN

According to NIMH statistics, eating disorders affect a small percentage: anorexia nervosa (0.5 to 3.7 percent), bulimia (1.1 to 4.2 percent) and binge-eating disorder (2 to 5 percent), but low percentages mean nothing if your daughter is suffering from one of these disorders. Teen girls who are deep into the neurotic behaviors of eating disorders need support to the fullest degree possible, including professional counseling for emotional and physical problems that can have life-threatening consequences. If you suspect your daughter has an eating disorder, get her to your primary care physician pronto for a referral to the appropriate professional. The physical consequences of eating disorders include irregular heartbeat, cardiac arrest, kidney and liver damage, destruction of teeth, loss of muscle mass, disruption of menstruation, infertility, permanent loss of bone mass, and death.

TREATMENT

Eating disorders differ from person to person, and treatment varies. However, treatment usually includes a full medical workup to determine what medications or supplements may be needed to restore health and balance. Amino acid supplementation is helpful. Individual, group, and/or family psychological counseling is usually part of the plan because depression, excessive anxiety, and low self-esteem are nearly always involved. Treatment may also include hospitalization or outpatient treatment, nutritional counseling, cognitive therapy, behavioral therapy, and, as a last resort, antidepressant medication.

WHAT MOMS CAN DO TODAY

1. Tell your daughter often that you love her, and let her know she is a unique and wonderful being. Don't stop telling her just because she's a teen. She may need to hear it now more than ever.

2. Educate her about her changing body and alleviate her fears.

3. Accept her appearance, and help her to do the same. Give continuing positive reinforcement.

4. Be a good role model by eating a healthy diet, maintaining a healthy weight, and getting plenty of exercise.

5. Be a good role model by accepting your own body, or if you are overweight, by adopting a healthy way of eating that leads to gradual and permanent weight loss, *not* by attempting to lose weight by severely restricting calories or obsessing about food.

6. Exercise with your daughter. Do fun activities together. Walk around the neighborhood, play active games, ride bikes, and go swimming. Even a stroll through the mall could be fun.

7. Provide healthy food choices and educate her about nutrition. Protein is brain and muscle food that helps girls stay smart, strong, and happy.

8. Protect her from lack of sleep, a high-sugar diet, and emotional stress.

9. Discuss with her the unrealistic female images on television and in magazines. How many "real" people does she know who are stick-thin and Angelina-gorgeous? Ask who among her daily contacts she admires and respects. Likely it will be a teacher or some other adult. Is that person physically perfect?

10. If she has gone from slender to scrawny, exercises obsessively, refuses to eat, or sends up other red flags associated with eating disorders, seek medical attention from a health-care professional who understands eating disorders and treats them often.

11. Consider having hormone levels tested, especially if her periods are irregular or she is missing periods. Often girls suffering from eating disorders do not ovulate regularly, leading to low progesterone levels, depression, and further eating abuse. Other tests that may be helpful include ferritin, CBC, and a chemistry screen to evaluate liver and kidney function levels.

— 8 —

PCOS—A NEW EPIDEMIC?

Polycystic Ovarian Syndrome (PCOS) affects between 5 percent and 10 percent of premenopausal girls and women, making it the most common hormonal problem among females of childbearing age. To a teen, it can be absolutely devastating. In the short term, it ruins her life. In the long term, it has far-reaching and potentially deadly consequences. Perhaps you have never heard of PCOS. Few adult women and even fewer teens have, but it is starting to gain notice in women's magazines. That's because it is on the rise, and it is affecting younger and younger women, including teens. It is quite probable that because so many girls and women are currently undiagnosed, an even higher percentage of females suffer from this complex and dangerous endocrine-metabolic disorder. Whatever the numbers, it is certain that millions of American women and girls have PCOS in varying degrees, and too many of them have been misdiagnosed or are undiagnosed. I see patients every week whose PCOS has been missed by other health professionals. Fifteen-year-old Cari was among them.

The first time I saw Cari, she was as unhappy and as scared as any teen I had ever seen. Her periods were irregular and were heavy and painful when she had one. She had rapidly gained weight, putting on fifty pounds in six months, and was now obese. She continued to gain weight despite the fact she was cutting calories. Most of the excess weight was in her upper body, especially her midsection. Cari was plagued by severe acne, and she had also developed dark facial and excess body hair, as well as velvety, discolored skin patches on her neck. The girl was miserable and felt like a freak.

Her pediatrician had been of no help. He said, correctly, that teens often have irregular periods and that acne is common. He also told her that her facial hair and weight gain were genetic, which could be true as her mother had type 2 diabetes, a metabolic disorder with some of the same underlying disorders as PCOS. He reassured Cari that her hormones would settle down in time, and she would get over her acne and painful periods. In the meantime, he advised her to adopt a low-fat diet and start an exercise program, which she did. (She continued to gain weight!)

Cari's mother had also taken her to a dietitian, the same dietitian who had advised the still-obese mother about her own diet. The dietitian dragged out the old food guide pyramid, reinforcing the pediatrician's advice, which was to use carbohydrates as the main floor of the diet by eating at least six to eleven daily servings of bread, bagels, pasta, rice, or cereal. Cari's carbohydrate cravings made adhering to the standard food guide pyramid relatively easy, even though she found it difficult to stay away from refined grains and sugar. But the carbs she was eating were low-fat, right? So why wasn't she losing weight? Why wasn't her complexion improving?

Cari's English teacher came to her rescue. The teacher's daughter had had PCOS, so she was familiar with the symptoms, all of which were apparent in Cari's weight, acne, facial hair, and skin discolorations. The teacher, who deserves a big hug, took Cari aside and recommended that she get an appointment at my women's hormone specialty clinic. It didn't take much for Cari to persuade her mother to make the call to my office—both were losing sleep over Cari's situation. One look at Cari and "PCOS" flashed in red letters on my mental diagnosis screen. I began describing to Cari and her mother the symptoms I suspected Cari must be having, and the mother broke into tears.

Am I smarter than the pediatrician and the dietitian—or a surprising number of medical professionals who miss this increasingly common and potentially deadly endocrine-metabolic disorder? Of course not. But I have specialized in hormone balancing for more than a decade, and I have seen too often the hallmarks of PCOS, all of which Cari had. I hope it won't be long before the mainstream medical world begins testing for and treating PCOS, which usually comes up as a probable cause of infertility when a woman reaches her late twenties or early thirties—after a lot of damage has already occurred. The incidence of PCOS is increasing right along with the national rise in obesity, insulin resistance, and diabetes. Leaving it undiagnosed and untreated will result in unnecessary heartbreak, disease, disability, infertility, and even premature death. PCOS must be addressed.

WHAT IS PCOS?

PCOS, first recognized in 1935, literally means *many ovarian cysts*, but it is much more than just a cluster of benign ovarian growths. PCOS is a complex and profound imbalance, a hormonal hurricane affecting not only the sex hormones but also the metabolism and the way the body handles blood sugar. Insulin resistance, when the body can't properly regulate blood sugar, is a key factor in most patients who have PCOS.

No one is sure exactly what causes PCOS. It may be a chicken-or-the-egg-situation. Many experts believe that insulin resistance is the trigger that begins a series of hormonal misfires that creates too much of some types of hormones and not enough of others. Insulin resistance fuels an upward spiral of midsection weight gain, which in turn results in abnormal cholesterol and triglyceride levels, abnormal reproductive function, and overproduction of male hormones, such as testosterone, by the adrenal glands. It is those male hormones that cause the acne and excess hairiness (hirsutism) common to PCOS.

OTHER CONTRIBUTING FACTORS

- Genetics may play a role. Daughters of mothers with PCOS are at greater risk. A shared diet and lifestyle may be as large a factor as genetic predisposition.
- Stress. Prolonged, everyday anxiety causes the adrenal glands to overproduce cortisol, which disrupts ovulation. Stress also steps up production of adrenal androgens.
- Lack of exercise. Being a sofa spud can contribute to insulin resistance and weight gain, leading to the hormonal disruptions characteristic of PCOS.
- Weight gain. Excess weight, often gained rapidly, is present in most but not all cases of PCOS. Being too heavy is associated with insulin resistance, which is characteristic of PCOS. Fat cells also produce estrone, a form of estrogen, which contributes to the imbalance.
- Bad diet. By "bad diet" I mean diets filled with hyper-processed, artificial junk, all the sugar-laden foods and drinks, artificially colored, flavored, and preserved rubbish that somehow qualifies as food. Continuing exposure to sugar and other refined white trash sets the stage for insulin resistance, from which numerous bad effects result. Diet can never really be separated from any health issue.
- Medications such as antidepressants may interfere with the hypothalamus, the master hormone center in the brain, and the normal firing of hormones.
- Birth control pills. Sometimes when girls stop using the pill, the hormone triangle from the brain to the ovaries and back to the brain does not reconnect, causing a loss of progesterone and triggering the vicious PCOS cycle. On the other hand, the pill is often effective in treating the period problems of PCOS because it shuts down the normal ovarian function and supplies hormones to create a menstrual cycle. There is no guarantee that the body will not revert to the bad cycle once the pill is stopped, however.

□ Chemicals in food. The average person consumes more than four pounds of food additives each year, some of them untested by the FDA. Meat animals are fed hormones and antibiotics, which persist in their flesh. Even some FDA-approved additives are controversial. Monosodium glutamate (MSG) is in most condiments, Chinese food, pickles, seasoning salts, soups, and baked goods; and aspartame (NutraSweet) is the artificial sweetener in diet soft drinks. These additives are among many that are under fire for suspected health risks. Food additives are another reason to avoid processed foods and—sorry—diet soft drinks.

□ Environmental chemicals. Chemical compounds, some of which imitate or block hormones in the body, are pervasive inside and outside of our homes. They are suspected of interfering with hormonal processes and may be contributing to PCOS, early puberty, and other hormonal disorders.

THE HEALTHY FEMALE CYCLE

A normal cycle depends upon a complex series of hormonal events. First, the hypothalamus, the hormonal master gland for reproduction, appetite, metabolism, and growth, releases gonadotropin-releasing hormone (GnRH) soon after the menstrual period ends each month. GnRH, in turn, stimulates the pituitary gland, located at the base of the brain just below the hypothalamus, to release follicle stimulating hormone (FSH) and luteinizing hormone (LH). These hormones order the ovaries to produce estrogen (estradiol) and stimulate the eggs inside the follicles to begin maturation. The egg released into the fallopian tube for a journey to the uterus changes its costume en route and becomes a "corpus luteum," a factory for the hormone progesterone. At this time, progesterone levels rise in the blood to be about three hundred times higher than estradiol levels. Estradiol is a type of estrogen.

The progesterone surge halts the egg-maturation process and initiates the thickening of the uterine lining to provide a rich nest in the event that the egg becomes fertilized. If pregnancy does not occur, the uterine lining sheds in a normal menstruation period, and the process begins again with a signal to the hypothalamus to release more GnRH.

PCOS DISRUPTS THE CYCLE

With PCOS, ovulation is almost always incomplete, which pitches a curve into the entire menstrual cycle. Rather than popping out of the follicle and traveling down the fallopian tube, the egg sticks to the outside of the ovary and forms a cyst. Month after month of this results in a "pearl necklace" of ovarian cysts, although this does not occur in every case. The cysts are relatively harmless. The problem is that when ovulation does not occur, progesterone is not made, and a nasty imbalance between estrogen and progesterone occurs. The ever-vigilant hypothalamus tries to put hormone levels back on an even keel by releasing more and more GnRH, which increases FSH and LH production. Too much LH and FSH result in overproduction of the male hormones, androgens, and free testosterone. Both the ovaries and the adrenal glands produce some testosterone in the female body normally, but too much creates problems. Hair follicles are sensitive to high testosterone levels, and acne, oily skin, and excess hair often develops.

All these disturbances are tied to insulin resistance, which, as we observed in Chapter 4, is also strongly linked to metabolic syndrome and type 2 diabetes. Insulin is a tissue-building (anabolic) hormone that builds fat and promotes fat storage. When there is too much insulin and glucose in the blood, cells may shut down and refuse to accept the glucose that the insulin is trying to deliver, sending the pancreas into even greater insulin production. Suddenly, the cells open up and suck in the excess glucose, which is stored as fat. Then low blood sugar occurs (hypoglycemia), triggering intense food cravings. If the person gives in to the craving, the whole process repeats.

Excess insulin, unstable blood glucose levels, and insulin resistance make the body a champion fat-storing unit. Increased fat heightens insulin resistance, and the person gets fatter and fatter in a brutal cycle that is difficult to break. With insulin resistance, you can actually eat less and gain weight.

PCOS SYMPTOMS

PCOS symptoms are not the same for everyone, but just about every female with the syndrome has irregular periods and/or painful periods, or no periods at all, after having had normal menstruation. The irregular period symptom is a tough one to recognize for younger teens, who may not have yet developed a regular cycle. It is not unusual for periods to be on-again, off-again for the first couple of years that a girl menstruates. If the period hasn't started by age sixteen, or if it has been unpredictable for more than two years, PCOS should be suspected, especially if accompanied by any of the following.

- Rapid weight gain, primarily around the middle and upper body.
- Obesity.
- Facial and/or excess body hair.
- Acne on face and often on other areas of the body.
- Heavy and painful periods—or missed or irregular periods.
- Lethargy.
- Depression.
- Lack of concentration and memory.
- Increased neck size.
- Masculine appearance.
- Pelvic pain.
- Velvety, hyper-pigmented skin folds.
- Male pattern baldness or thinning hair.
- Multiple ovarian cysts and enlarged ovaries.

Since so few mothers and even fewer teens seem to know about PCOS, they may see a doctor for reasons associated with PCOS symptoms without knowing about the syndrome itself. Menstrual problems are the most common reason for seeking medical attention, with excess hair growth, acne, and obesity not far behind. The sooner the syndrome is arrested, the better. PCOS may begin gradually with a few symptoms that teens may shrug off. But teens with full-tilt PCOS will have a difficult time ignoring it, and even mild PCOS can be devastating to health.

Diagnosing PCOS can be a challenge because it presents so differently from one female to the next. Perhaps that's why so many physicians fail to diagnose it. Not every patient is a cut-and-dried example like Cari. Only about half of the girls with PCOS will show positive signs of cysts with a pelvic ultrasound scan. Hormone level tests can help to pinpoint the syndrome. In general, a patient with PCOS will have characteristic abnormal hormone levels, which usually include an imbalance between progesterone (too low) and estradiol (too low or high), and abnormally high total and free testosterone levels. A thyroid panel, DHEA-S, FSH, LH, SHBG, fasting glucose and insulin levels, and a comprehensive metabolic panel will likely also reveal abnormalities.

LONG-TERM HEALTH RISKS

PCOS makes a mess of a girl's immediate life—acne, obesity, hairiness, and painful, irregular periods are tough conditions to deal with for even the most well-adjusted girl—but the long-term risks are even more troubling. PCOS creates a significant increased risk for type 2 diabetes, cardiovascular disease, hypertension, and uterine, ovarian, and breast cancer. It is also a major cause of infertility.

The acne with PCOS is especially severe and often affects not only the face but also the neck, shoulders, and upper arms. A girl with undiagnosed PCOS, who is being treated for acne, will not see much, if any, improvement. The entire syndrome must be treated to avoid long-term problems such as scarring.

TREATING PCOS NATURALLY

As is the case with most hormonal disorders, there is no one-plan-works-for-all remedy. Each patient has a different set of symptoms and reacts differently to treatment, so there can be a fair amount of trial and error. I use a combination of approaches to treat PCOS, beginning with diet—the simplest yet one of the most complex approaches. Without permanent dietary improvements, which include sharply reducing or eliminating sugar and refined grains, symptoms will continue and long-term medical problems are likely to develop. Other natural approaches include the following:

1. Micronized progesterone. The use of bioidentical progesterone ranks in importance with dietary improvements, and I usually prescribe it orally or topically fourteen days before the period is to begin. Not all medical providers agree with this treatment. However, the lack of complete ovulation with PCOS means the body is not manufacturing its own progesterone. During normal ovulation, progesterone levels are three hundred times higher than at other times during the cycle, and this fact should not be ignored. Not only low estrogen signals the hypothalamus to make GnRH and perpetuate the normal reproductive cycle, but also progesterone does. Synthetic progesterone (progestins) such as Provera, Aygestin, or the birth-control pill should not be substituted for bioidentical progesterone, as they do not come close to duplicating the body's progesterone.

2. Exercise. Regular exercise helps to increase insulin sensitivity and promotes weight loss.

3. Stress management. Relieving stress can cut back on cortisol, an adrenal hormone, which contributes to the acne and hairiness of PCOS.

THE PCOS-CORRECTING DIET

The PCOS-Correcting Diet could be called the Insulin-Glucose Balancing Diet because the aim is to get the body's cells sensitized to insulin again, and the way to do that is by depriving the body of what it craves—sugar and starch. The PCOS-Correcting Diet is low in carbohydrates and high in protein and good fats. It is high in fiber, contains ample omega-3 fatty acids, and includes soy products and ground flaxseed meal or flaxseed oil.

Here's the scoop on sugar. It isn't just that white stuff that is dumped by the truckloads into cakes and cookies, sodas and ice cream. All carbohydrates, even brown rice, apples, and whole wheat bread, eventually turn into simple glucose in the bloodstream. (*Eventually* is the operative word here.) Once glucose is in the bloodstream, the insulin-resistant cells don't have a clue whether it came from white sugar, an orange, or a whole grain cracker. All they know is that insulin is knocking on the door with a load of glucose, and they've had it with glucose and are putting up the locks and bolts!

The trick when trying to reverse insulin resistance is to increase protein, reduce carbohydrates, and include good, satisfying fats such as olive oil, nuts, seeds, and avocados. It is absolutely essential to banish refined carbohydrates such as sugar, white bread, bagels, pasta, pretzels, white flour tortillas, crackers, chips, cookies, cakes, sugary cereals, ice cream, and so on. I am not suggesting giving up carbs altogether. Just choose wisely. Think *whole* when selecting grains, fruits, and vegetables, which all contain carbohydrates.

According to the rules of the glycemic index described in Chapter 7, the less processing a food has been subjected to, the longer it takes for the body to break it down into simple sugar. That longer processing time prevents blood sugar spikes. When you eat a slice of bread made from a refined grain, a piece of cake, or, unfortunately, even a potato, the bloodstream gets slammed with a wave of glucose that peaks like a tsunami. High levels of insulin and glucose rampage in the bloodstream, and the excess insulin causes glucose to be stored as fat instead of used for quick energy. Then because cells aren't actually getting enough energy, you feel ravenous, especially for carbohydrates, and eat even more, getting fatter by the minute and perpetuating this ugly cycle.

When you eat a whole-grain, low-carbohydrate tortilla (such as Tumaro's Gourmet Tortillas) and top it with peanut butter or a bit of cream cheese, the body has to work harder to separate the fiber from the grain and digest the protein and fat in the peanut butter or cream cheese. Your body gets a steady supply of glucose rather than an onslaught, insulin and glucose levels begin to stabilize, and insulin resistance is reduced.

SUPPLEMENTS AND HERBS TO TREAT PCOS

The following supplements are encouraged for girls with PCOS and can be taken according to package recommendations. Always inform your health-care provider about supplements being used.

- Evening primrose oil, 500–1200 mg daily
- Calcium, magnesium, zinc
- Selenium
- Chromium picolinate, 400–600 mcg daily in divided doses
- L-glutamine for blood sugar regulation and craving reduction, 500 mg twice daily on empty stomach
- Coenzyme Q10
- Vitamins B_6, C, and E
- Green tea

The following supplements and herbs should be used under the direction of a naturopath or other medical professional knowledgeable in their effects.

- Taurine
- Infusion therapy for minerals, vitamins, and amino acid support

□ Biotin

□ Alpha/lipoic acid

□ Gymnema

□ Fenugreek

□ Bitter melon

□ Devil's club

□ Jambool

□ Saw palmetto

□ Nettles

□ Chaste tree berry

□ Acidophilus

Glucophage/Metformin is a prescription medicine used to treat high insulin levels. It depletes folic acid and B_{12} so be sure to supplement these vitamins if it is prescribed. Do not combine with ginkgo biloba.

OTHER PCOS TREATMENTS

Prescription medications can be useful in treating PCOS, especially insulin-sensitizing medications such as those containing the drug *metformin*, which is commonly prescribed for diabetic patients. Metformin helps to reverse insulin resistance, reduce free testosterone levels, restore the menstrual cycle, reverse hairiness, and reduce weight. Avandia and Actos are other diabetes drugs that may be prescribed for PCOS. All these medications have side effects that may include diarrhea, nausea, vomiting, abdominal bloating, gas, and loss of appetite. It is wise to start with a very small dose and then increase the dose, spreading it throughout the day, or taking a time-release capsule in the morning and the afternoon. It is also important to follow the dietary recommendations and to eat regular meals. These drugs have built-in accountability, because if you eat junk food with them or skip meals, you just don't feel very well. Other treatments include:

□ **Birth-control pills.** The use of the pill is a possibility for the teen girl. It will provide some health benefits, such as normalizing the period, increasing a hormone called sex-hormone-binding globulin (SHBG), which reduces circulating testosterone, the hormone that causes acne, oily skin, and hair on the face and body.

□ **Anti-androgens.** Medications that lower testosterone are called anti-androgens. Options include Spirinolactone (Aldactone), Flutamide, Cyproterone Acetate, and Finasteride. These medications may be used to control facial and body hair, reduce acne, restore the hair that has been lost on the head, and normalize testosterone levels. Side effects may include irregular bleeding, nausea, fatigue, and indigestion.

No matter what the treatment, regular medical checkups are essential when being treated for PCOS. Periodic evaluations will let the medical practitioner know how the body is responding and whether medications should be adjusted.

PCOS, METABOLIC SYNDROME, INSULIN RESISTANCE, AND DIABETES

You probably have noticed by now the common threads linking PCOS, diabetes, metabolic syndrome, and insulin resistance. All are serious hormonal and metabolic disruptions, and PCOS and insulin resistance are strong risk factors for developing type 2 diabetes. In addition, all are major body fat promoters. The good news is that if PCOS, metabolic syndrome, and insulin resistance are addressed early, type 2 diabetes can be prevented. Treating any of these conditions helps to address the others. The importance of proper diet and regular exercise cannot be overemphasized.

WHAT MOMS CAN DO TODAY

1. Learn the symptoms of PCOS. If you suspect PCOS is plaguing your daughter, bring the symptom list when she sees a doctor and make sure she is tested correctly.
2. Say good-bye to sugar, white flour and other refined foods high on the glycemic index. These foods are poison to your daughter and aren't good for anyone else in the family either. Involve the entire family in healthier eating.
3. Don't store hot food in plastic, heat leftovers in plastic containers, or serve coffee or tea in plastic cups. Toxic chemicals leached from plastics can contain estrogen-like compounds that can create or complicate hormone imbalance.
4. Stock up on healthy snacks such as berries (fresh, frozen, or dried—no sugar), nuts, jerky, and other low GI foods. Veggies and dips are good choices. Try a hummus or other dip found in the health food section of most grocery stores.
5. Stay involved in your daughter's care. At follow-up visits, look to see that she is losing weight or body fat and showing improvement in her lab tests, that medications are being tailored to her specific needs and test levels, and that she is getting the medical support she needs to overcome PCOS symptoms.
6. Insist on the best care for her. If she is not being helped, consider going to our Web site, www.hormonesinbalance.com, for more information and consultation.

7. If medications have been prescribed for her, make sure she takes them faithfully. If she is having difficulty with consistency or is not tolerating medications well, see the medical expert soon.

8. Help her to chart her menstrual cycle. Once treatment begins, periods should begin to be more regular, less painful, and lighter.

9. Make sure she eats a hearty breakfast that includes at least fourteen grams of protein. One large egg contains 6.25 grams of protein, so two eggs and a slice of lean ham would be adequate.

10. Encourage exercise, and join her if that will help to motivate her.

11. L-glutamine, 1,000 mg; flaxseed oil, 2,000 mg; and chromium, 400 mcg, taken at breakfast will help to control her carbohydrate cravings.

9

PMS—
PRETTY MEAN STUFF

Fifteen-year-old Ellie appeared in my office with her mother, Karen, who had practically dragged the girl through the door. Karen was clearly at her wit's end. She reported that Ellie was missing school a day or two each month due to period problems, and that she was moody, depressed, and outrageously short-tempered in the days before her period. Oh, and by the way, she admitted, "I am sort of moody and depressed myself."

What could be worse than one person in a household suffering from premenstrual syndrome (PMS)? That's easy—*two* people. Moms and their daughters are often in sync with their periods, and if Mom suffers from any degree of PMS, chances are so does her daughter. The resulting decline in household civility can set the entire family on edge for several days each month.

Since I specialize in hormone balancing, Karen hoped that I would prescribe natural hormones, antidepressants, or *something* to mellow-out her daughter's PMS. Whoa. Not so fast. First we needed to determine if Ellie's symptoms resulted from PMS and, if so, then both mother and daughter needed some basic education about this oh-so-common female affliction.

PMS is associated with more than 150 symptoms. In all my years of treating women, I have yet to find two with the same set of PMS symptoms and none with the same reaction to the symptoms. Typically, however, PMS symptoms occur in relation to the monthly cycle. The most common pattern is that the symptoms appear in the last days leading up to the next period. They may last one day or up to twenty-one days, and may come and go. The problems may arise around the time of ovulation (the midpoint between periods) and then stop, only to reappear right before the period begins. PMS symptoms sometimes skip a month or two but are recurrent.

PMS symptoms are divided into three categories: mental, emotional, and physical. Emotional and mental symptoms may include sadness and depression, anger and rage, irritability, tension, anxiety, restlessness, lack of focus, and irrationality. The physical symptoms can include fatigue, weight gain and bloating, acne, oily skin, headaches, muscle aches, appetite changes, food cravings, binges, loss of coordination, recurrent yeast or bladder infections, and more. That's a lot of discord and misery, but it doesn't have to be that way.

TESTING AND TREATING

Ellie exhibited several classic PMS symptoms—moodiness, bloating, and irritability in the days before her period. Indeed, when Ellie and I sat down with a calendar, she was able to correlate her school absences, behavior, and physical symptoms with where she was in her cycle. Looking back, she saw that her crying jags, foul temper, food cravings, bloating, and fatigue occurred most often during the week before her period. Once her period began, the symptoms disappeared and she forgot about them—until next time. Any female who has black and white mood swings related to her period is most likely suffering from PMS, and so was Ellie. Unfortunately, so was her mom.

In most cases, if a patient has had PMS symptoms for three months or longer, I order a hormone profile, primarily to test for progesterone deficiency, but also to look at estrogen, testosterone, and other levels. I also order tests to rule out anemia and low thyroid. Treating with hormones is not always the first line of offense, but determining hormone levels at the critical part of the cycle is an essential diagnostic tool.

But the situation was far from hopeless. At least half of what I do in my practice is educate women, and sometimes men, about the links between whatever physical and emotional symptoms they are experiencing and their diets, stress, sleep patterns, and exercise levels. Now hear this: poor diet, toxic stress, inadequate rest, and physical inactivity lead to hormonal imbalances and disease. They also make PMS worse.

Ellie's diet was the all-too-typical teen fare—heavy on sugar and refined junk and light on fresh veggies, whole grains, quality protein, and fruit. She was stressed out with family issues, including her monthly blow-ups with her mom, and by school, where she had a hard time focusing. She tended to read and watch television rather than use her leisure time in physical activity, and she was getting only six or seven hours of sleep a night, inadequate for a teen. I suggested to Ellie that changing a few habits could help her get rid of the donut she was accumulating around her middle, balance her moods throughout the month, provide her with pep, vim, and vigor, and make her life a whole lot easier for the next thirty-five or so years she could expect to be menstruating. Was she ready for that? "Okay," said Ellie. "Let's go for it."

PMS TREATMENT OPTIONS

Before any treatment begins, everybody in the household needs to recognize that PMS is real. PMS is a "whole body" hormonal imbalance, and labeling it as "just a bad mood" does a disservice to those who suffer from it. Dismissing your daughter's short temper, weepiness, or physical maladies with offhand remarks, such as, "Oh, she's just on the rag" or "Aunt Flow must be coming," should be discouraged. Instead, cooperate to reduce stressors during the difficult days of the month and to implement lifestyle changes that are likely to ease or eliminate her symptoms. The simple recommendations below can change the course of your daughter's mental, physical, and emotional future. (And your's too!)

1. Reduce stress. Try to minimize stress-causing situations or excessive exposure to negative personality types. Help your daughter to set priorities, cut back on obligations, and relax.

2. Get moving. Regular exercise has a profound effect on mood and overall health. Help her to develop a plan for getting fresh air and exercise daily.

3. Clean up the diet. Getting adequate nutrition is essential to optimal health, and eliminating blood sugar peaks and valleys is the key to stabilizing mood and keeping energy up. Maintaining that stability and getting adequate nutrients means:

- Eating small, frequent meals throughout the day and including protein in each.
- Avoiding sugary, highly processed and refined foods.
- Eating whole grains.
- Including four to six servings of fruits and vegetables daily.
- Drinking lots of water.
- Avoiding salty foods that can cause water retention and bloating.

Finally, here's a PMS treatment that everybody likes: eat a little chocolate—the darker and more concentrated, the better. Chocolate can increase serotonin levels in the brain, which ultimately improves mood. Real chocolate also contains theobromine, which is similar to caffeine and can temporarily boost energy. I suggest savoring a couple of pieces of good dark chocolate prior to the period. Pay attention to the amount because, unfortunately, chocolate is approximately 50 percent fat and 50 percent sugar. You can definitely get too much of a good thing.

PROGESTERONE THERAPY

Whenever a female of any age has had PMS symptoms for three months or longer, I order a hormone profile to test for progesterone deficiency and other hormone imbalances. If the above recommendations are ineffective after three months and PMS continues to steal several days a month, progesterone therapy may be in order. Natural progesterone therapy just works! The majority of women of all ages whom I see for depression and PMS have low circulating levels of progesterone. It is interesting to note that PMS most often occurs in the second half of the menstrual cycle, which is when progesterone levels are supposed to be highest. But when ovulation does not occur, as it often doesn't in teens, the usual progesterone surge does not occur either, and estrogen circulates unopposed. The red light blinks: hormone imbalance! PMS!

HORMONE TESTING AND TREATING WITH HORMONES

Before prescribing progesterone, it is necessary to test the levels in the blood. Of utmost importance, the testing should be done in the two weeks before the period, which is the luteal phase of the cycle when progesterone is being secreted during ovulation.

Natural progesterone absorbs well through the skin, as do many other hormones and medications. It can also be prescribed as a sublingual lozenge, tablet, drop, capsule, or vaginal suppository. I usually recommend taking progesterone from day fourteen of the cycle to the twenty-eighth day, but this can vary. It is important to use the progesterone faithfully so irregular bleeding does not occur.

Below are recommended options for use of progesterone therapy.

- Progesterone time-release capsules—100 mg/day taken 1 to 2 times per day. These are oral micronized progesterone capsules in an oil base.
- Progesterone sublingual drops or troches—50–100 mg–2 times per day for symptom relief.

□ Progesterone transdermal creams—over-the-counter or prescription doses can be used and are taken in the amount that relieves symptoms. Over-the-counter doses typically are 20–40 mg twice daily.

ANTIDEPRESSANTS

Antidepressants are definitely not my first line of treatment. I believe that the majority of PMS symptoms can be dramatically improved with diet, supplements, exercise, and, if relief is not evident, progesterone therapy. However, using prescription antidepressants is important for teens who have tried everything and are still suffering with severe symptoms, including suicidal impulses. Antidepressant drugs, such as Prozac, do not relieve physical PMS symptoms. If you believe that your daughter's mood disorder goes beyond PMS, I recommend that you seek help from a mental health professional.

DIAGNOSING PMS

The first step in diagnosing PMS is to keep a calendar of symptoms as they correlate to the menstrual cycle. This is useful *before* working with a medical provider who is skilled in diagnosing and treating PMS. (For more on menstrual charting, see Chapter 12.) Your provider will rule out, as I did with Ellie, conditions such as anemia, thyroid deficiency, diabetes, clinical depression, or chronic fatigue. Other conditions to be ruled out include candida, endometriosis, and autoimmune disorders such as chronic fatigue or fibromyalgia.

Some women/girls have what is known as extreme PMS, when symptoms may include seizures, migraine headaches, severe depression, sleep problems, irritable bowel problems, and asthma. These symptoms are relatively rare, however. The criteria for a formal PMS diagnosis are stringent and include that the symptoms be present for at least one year. In my office, however, we diagnose and treat prior to allowing problems to continue—and girls and women to suffer—for months on end.

PMS ASSESSMENT CHECKLIST

1. Do you experience the following mood changes?

BEFORE PERIOD	2–3 WEEKS PER MONTH	ALL MONTH	
☐	☐	☐	Anger
☐	☐	☐	Irritability
☐	☐	☐	Depression
☐	☐	☐	Erratic moods
☐	☐	☐	Crying spells

2. Do you experience the following physical changes?

BEFORE PERIOD	2–3 WEEKS PER MONTH	ALL MONTH	
☐	☐	☐	Weight gain
☐	☐	☐	Breast tenderness
☐	☐	☐	Hair loss
☐	☐	☐	Low-back pain
☐	☐	☐	Ovarian pain
☐	☐	☐	Hands/feet swelling
☐	☐	☐	Dry skin
☐	☐	☐	Headaches
☐	☐	☐	Constipation

3. Do you experience the following in your behavior?

BEFORE PERIOD	2–3 WEEKS PER MONTH	ALL MONTH	
☐	☐	☐	Increased food cravings
☐	☐	☐	Fatigue
☐	☐	☐	Forgetfulness
☐	☐	☐	Insomnia
☐	☐	☐	Lack of coordination
☐	☐	☐	Indecision

If your daughter experiences at least four of the symptoms listed above and has them prior to her period, she is probably suffering from PMS. If she experiences ten or more symptoms, it is likely that PMS is significantly altering her life. The number of days that symptoms are present is also important. If symptoms last more than five days per month, testing and treatment should be sought.

WHAT CAUSES PMS?

PMS cannot be pinned on any one cause but is likely the result of numerous factors. One theory is that symptoms are triggered by a disruption in, or lack of, the brain neurotransmitters that stabilize mood. Neurotransmitters such as serotonin can be depleted, which may lead to the emotional and sometimes physical complaints of PMS. Another theory is that an estrogen/progesterone imbalance contributes to PMS symptoms. Teens typically have irregular ovulation, especially during the first two years of menstruation, and progesterone is produced primarily by the ovaries at the time of ovulation. (It is also made in small amounts by the adrenal glands.) When ovulation fails to occur, progesterone levels drop and estrogen dominates, often resulting in mood swings. It is believed that the following factors contribute to PMS:

1. Stress. Causes an elevation of stress hormones, which can disrupt estrogen and progesterone levels. Stress can also reduce the body's ability to respond to progesterone.

2. Diet high in sugar and refined, highly processed grains. Leads to elevated insulin, which sets up an imbalance in the estrogen-progesterone ratio. Diet can also activate stress hormones leading to deactivation of the progesterone receptors. Current research indicates that women who eat a high-sugar diet have an increased incidence of PMS. High amounts of caffeine and alcohol are also associated with an increased incidence.

3. Inadequate sleep. Contributes to a myriad of complaints, including a loss of precious brain chemicals normally made during sleep, leading to elevated stress hormones that cause fatigue, irritability, and brain fog.

4. Serotonin (neurotransmitter) drop. Associated with mood imbalance, may cause depression.

5. Vitamin deficiencies. Can aggravate or promote PMS symptoms. (Lack of B$_6$, calcium, magnesium, manganese, and vitamin E)

6. Genetics. Predisposition to PMS may be passed from mother to daughter.

7. Low thyroid function. Restoring thyroid hormone levels to normal ranges can significantly reduce, or eliminate, PMS symptoms.

SUPPLEMENTS TO HELP ALLEVIATE PMS

- Evening primrose oil (EPO) capsules: Several studies have shown the effectiveness of EPO in treating PMS. EPO contains an essential fatty acid that helps promote prostaglandin, which inhibits the action of prolactin. Prolactin is found in high levels in women with PMS and can cause progesterone levels to drop. The use of EPO can help reverse this process and promote well-being. It is additionally helpful for menstrual cramps and heavy bleeding.
- Vitamin D with calcium and magnesium: Calcium and magnesium can significantly aid in sleep when taken in the evening. Recent studies have shown an improvement in PMS symptoms with the use of calcium supplements. Vitamin D has been shown through the research of endocrinologist Robert Fredericks, MD, to have a positive effect in regulating energy metabolism.[1] The dose should be 500–1200 mg of calcium with magnesium daily. In our office we

use a liquid cal/mag that is extremely well absorbed and helpful for symptom relief.

☐ B complex: B complex is a "stress vitamin complex" that can help improve the body's response to stress by relieving cravings and joint and muscle pain, and increasing energy, mental concentration, and memory. In my office we use a sublingual preparation of this complex that is adequately absorbed and excellent for a PMS pickup.

☐ Herbs such as licorice root, wild yam root, astralagus, dong quai, ginger, vitex, burdock root, motherwort, horsetail, and red clover can be helpful in treating PMS. I suggest an herbal combination of some of these in a tincture form that is fresh and high grade.

☐ L-tyrosine and L-phenylalaline. These amino acids can be extremely helpful for the treatment of depression and low moods. They should be started in low doses and used regularly for two months in order to evaluate the effects.

☐ 5-HTP: 50–100 mg of this once or twice daily can improve the mood and provide excellent sleep quality.

The above supplements are what I prescribe to most of my PMS patients.

WHAT MOMS CAN DO TODAY

1. Teach your daughter that PMS symptoms can be relieved. Don't believe that having PMS is just something to put up with.
2. You have heard this before: get rid of the junk in the cupboard and refrigerator and provide nutritious meals and snacks.
3. Don't tolerate trash talk that puts down everything a teen does because she's having her period or is about to.
4. Enforce the eight-hours-a-night rule for sleep, and nine is better.
5. Increase the fiber in the diet. This will help with estrogen metabolism and reduce estrogen dominance. Veggies, whole grains, or just adding two tablespoons of psyllium husks to the morning drink or oatmeal will add significant fiber.
6. Ask for hormone testing. Be sure to request progesterone, estradiol, free testosterone, and thyroid levels in the second half of the monthly cycle.
7. If hormone testing is not available locally, visit my Web site, www.hormonesinbalance.com.
8. Start your daughter as soon as possible on daily calcium-magnesium, vitamin D, evening primrose oil, and a B complex. This will not only provide excellent treatment for PMS, but these supplements are great for brain, bones, muscles, weight, and skin. They will also provide a wonderful jump start to the treatment program. Stay on these for a minimum of three months.

9. Help your daughter increase her physical activity. This will boost brain serotonin levels, ease irritability, and provide improved mood and better hormone and blood sugar balance.

10. Help your daughter manage her stress before her period begins. Reducing extra responsibilities and pressure four to seven days prior will create less havoc with PMS. Stress heightens PMS.

11. Assist your daughter in charting her symptoms. This will help her to get the right treatment and to identify what her PMS triggers may be.

12. Be good to her. Offer the essentials: back rubs, lavender baths, long walks, extra help with her homework, chamomile tea, and other evidence of your motherly love. This will not only help her in the moment, but will teach her how to take care of herself. Just as important, it will help her to acknowledge her personal needs and understand that her monthly "times" are not a joke. This is really important!

10

SEX—TEENS DON'T HAVE TO GIVE IT AWAY

Kelly was sixteen when she first had sex with Rob, a popular jock who was two years older. Her parents didn't have a clue that their church-going daughter was sexually active, and Rob's parents were also in the dark. The lusty teens often spent hours in Rob's locked downstairs bedroom while his oblivious parents, upstairs watching television, told themselves that the kids were "just listening to music." Rob pressured Kelly by saying he would find another girlfriend if she didn't sleep with him.

For the next year, Kelly had frequent unprotected sex with Rob, got pregnant, had a secret abortion, contracted herpes (Rob had other sexual partners), and prayed to God for forgiveness. Kelly's parents were churchgoing people who did not invite discussion about anything they considered immoral, which would have included most of what Kelly was doing in her secret life. Kelly continued to attend church and presented a façade of chastity, but inside she was crumbling and confused. It never occurred to Kelly to approach her mother about sex, and her mother never brought up the subject.

I first saw Kelly in my medical office when she was the mother of a two-year-old daughter, with whom Kelly vows to have a continuing discussion about all that matters, including sex. She doesn't want to make the same mistakes with her child that her parents, especially her mother, made with her. And she sure doesn't want her daughter to be used sexually the way she was.

Kelly's story may be extreme, but then again, perhaps not. After talking with numerous sexually active teens and grown women looking back on their teen sexual experiences, I know that girls who have sex before they are emotionally ready can suffer a range of consequences that includes not only pregnancies, abortions, and sexually transmitted diseases, but troubled relationships with men in general and long-term struggles with self-worth. I have to hold myself back from grabbing my teen patients by the shoulders and begging them to stop having sex, or to abstain if they haven't already started. I applaud peer-taught abstinence-based pregnancy prevention programs and the virginity pledge movement, which at least one study, the National Longitudinal Study of Adolescent Health, shows reduces the probability that an adolescent will begin sexual activity compared with her peers. (Data from the same study, reported in the *Journal of Adolescent Health*, showed that teens who took abstinence pledges had the same rate of STDs as those who did not, possibly because, when they had sex, nonpledgers did not use condoms at sexual debut.)[1] But here's another, more promising finding: when taking a virginity pledge is combined with strong parental disapproval of sexual activity, the probability of initiation of sexual activity is reduced by 75 percent or more.[2]

We must let our daughters know that playing with sex is playing with fire. To parody a line from a Willie Nelson tune, "Mothers, don't let your babies grow up to be sex toys."

IS YOUR DAUGHTER HAVING SEX?

Before you say, "Not my child," remember how oblivious Kelly's (and Rob's) parents were, and consider these facts from the National Campaign to Prevent Teen Pregnancy:

- About one in five teens has had sexual intercourse before age fifteen.
- One in seven sexually experienced fourteen-year-old girls has been pregnant.
- About half of fourteen-year-olds say they have attended parties with no adult supervision.
- Only about a third of parents of sexually experienced fourteen-year-olds know that their children are having sex.[3]

These astounding facts are from the Alan Guttmacher Institute, a Washington-based nonprofit research group:

- By their eighteenth birthday, six in ten teen women and nearly seven in ten teen men have had sexual intercourse.
- A sexually active teen who does not use contraception has a 90 percent chance of becoming pregnant within a year.
- Of the approximately 950,000 teen pregnancies that occur each year, more than three in four are unintended. Over one quarter of these pregnancies end in abortion.
- The pregnancy rate among US women ages 15 to 19 has declined steadily—from 117 pregnancies per 1,000 women in 1990 to 93 per 1,000 women in 1997. Analysis of the teen pregnancy rate decline between 1988 and 1995 found that approximately one-quarter of the decline was due to delayed onset of sexual inter-course among teens, while three-quarters was due to the increased use of highly effective and long-acting contraceptive methods among sexually experienced teens.
- Despite the decline, the United States continues to have one of the highest teen pregnancy rates in the developed world—twice as high as those in England, Wales, or Canada and nine times as high as rates in the Netherlands and Japan.
- Every year, roughly four million new sexually transmitted disease (STD) infections occur among teens in the United States.

Compared with rates among teens in other developed countries, rates of gonorrhea and chlamydia among U.S teens are extremely high.[4]

PLEASE TELL HER SHE CAN SAY NO

Parents need to start early telling girls the truth about sex: you don't have to give it away, and you are not ready for what it can do to your head, let alone to your body. Even when kids get into those powerful first-love relationships that they are sure will last forever, they need to know that *sex does not have to be part of the deal.* It most cases it complicates, rather than deepens, a relationship. I have seen too many abandoned girls with sadness in their eyes and emptiness in their hearts—not to mention sexually transmitted diseases (STDs) and unwanted pregnancies.

It is challenging in our sex-saturated culture to promote the idea that teens should postpone sex. We hardly even blink at thirteen-year-olds parading around in revealing camisoles, and we are numb, almost, to the undulating bodies on music videos and to gratuitous and graphic sex in movies and, increasingly, on prime-time television. It seems that most girls are either incredibly naïve about the effect that their sexy clothing has on males or are using their sexuality to get attention. Either way, skin-tight T-shirts, bare midriffs, and hip-hugging, low-slung pants invite men to take the next mental step by imagining the body parts that aren't showing. Do young girls know this? Would they dress this suggestively and saunter around in their I'm-looking-for-sex type outfits if they knew the fantasies they incite in men of all ages, shapes, and sizes? With Britney Spears, Christina Aguilera, and Paris Hilton as role models, how are teen girls supposed to think that modesty is good and virginity is smart? Sex is so pervasive in pop culture that too many teens advertise by their clothing that they want it and accept it as inevitable. It isn't a matter of waiting for the right guy or the culmination of a long-term commitment or, heaven forbid, marriage, but something to say you have done. Something that you have to do to fit in. Something that is expected. This has to change!

Even though most teens know a peer who has been dumped by a sex partner, had a baby or an abortion or perhaps even an STD, the it-won't-happen-to-me syndrome prevails. Of course, it *can* happen to them and does. I have spent hours in my office counseling girls who have been walked all over by boys who were suddenly "done" with them. Or even if it was the girl's choice to move on, she was left with the emotional baggage of a sexual relationship for which she was not prepared—and sometimes a whole lot more.

YOU'RE GOING OUT DRESSED LIKE THAT?!

I am appalled at the leave-nothing-to-the-imagination, clingy, sexy, transparent outfits that are worn by teens. Parents who haven't abdicated their responsibility are still barricading the door as their young would-be sex sirens attempt to leave the home in outfits meant for Barbie. Unfortunately, anger, lecturing, and locking them up doesn't work. Super-revealing sexy outfits are in fashion, but more modest clothing is also in style, and you can help her to choose wisely. Try this experiment: Take her to the mall and have a seat. Then watch the people, especially men or teen boys, who are people watching. Observe them as they leer at the passing parade. Does your daughter want to be the object of ogling or the focus of the inevitable rating and berating that goes on? She may sneer at this exercise, but her consciousness may raise a tick.

If you find that your daughter enjoys the attention she gets from parading in ultrasexy outfits, it might be time to question why she needs this type of attention. Is there room at home for more positive attention from the family?

ARE YOU READY FOR THIS?

Don't look now, but oral sex is a growing trend among teens. In fact, according to a groundbreaking study by the Centers for Disease Control and Prevention based on 2002 data and released in October 2005, 28 percent of guys ages fifteen to seventeen reported giving oral sex to a female, and 40 percent report receiving it. Among girls of the same ages, 30 percent reported giving oral sex, and 38 percent said they received it.[5] A sex act once reserved for intimate, long-term relationships has become common. A big problem is that many teens think that oral sex isn't really sex! Teens tend to view oral sex as less intimate than vaginal sex, unlike mature women who see oral sex as part of a well-developed, long-term sexual and emotional relationship. They also see it as safer than vaginal sex, and the idea of using condoms or, God forbid, dental dams, during oral sex just doesn't play well in the steamed-up backseat or behind the locked bedroom door where the kids are "just listening to music."

Teens know about the pregnancy risks associated with intercourse, but you can't get pregnant performing oral sex, right? And you won't get an STD, either. At least that's what a lot of teens believe. According to writer Lisa Remez, whose special report "Oral Sex Among Adolescents: Is It Sex, or Is It Abstinence?" appeared in the journal *Family Planning Perspectives*, "There is growing evidence, although still anecdotal and amassed largely by journalists, not researchers, that adolescents might be turning to behaviors that avoid pregnancy risk but leave them vulnerable to acquisition of many STDs, including HIV."[6] These behaviors include mutual masturbation, oral sex, and anal intercourse.

What's the harm in a little oral sex? In the words of a twentysomething looking back on her teen years: "I am pretty sure no one thinks of oral sex as sex and that very few kids know the risks associated with the act. I also know that kids rarely use any protection. Oral sex is a status symbol for guys. I remember this girl showed up for school one Monday after breaking up with her boyfriend, and he had written all over the lockers, in crass language, that she had given him oral sex. It was terrible. The girls laughed at her and called her a slut, and so did the guys."

Aside from a trashed reputation, humiliation, and being exploited, the fallout from oral sex can be more tangible; many STDs can be transmitted orally. Transmitting HIV this way is relatively rare, but other STDs that can be contracted through oral sex include human papillomavirus (HPV), herpes simplex virus, hepatitis B, gonorrhea, syphilis, chlamydia, and chancroid.

STDs contracted orally present with oral symptoms. If a girl contracts genital herpes doing oral sex, she'll get herpes blisters in her mouth. If she contracts gonorrhea, she'll develop the infection in her throat. And so on. She needs to know.

STDs

"Sorry, dear, but you've got herpes," are among the most unpleasant and common words I have uttered to some of my young patients. For herpes, substitute human papillomavirus (HPV—genital warts), chlamydia, or one of twenty-some other STDs that regularly show up in sexually active young people. Teens are invariably shocked and "totally can't believe it" that the guy (or guys) who swore to be "clean" were not. In many cases, the partner didn't realize he had one or more STDs. Several common STDs, including gonorrhea, chlamydia, and HPV, may not cause symptoms at first, but, if untreated, can lead to various infections and infertility, or, in the case of HPV, precancerous or cancerous cell changes.

I can't stress strongly enough how prevalent these infections are and *how easy they are to contract.* All it takes is one sexual encounter. Teens must remember that if they are having unprotected sex, they aren't having sex with just one person but with every other person that their partner has had sex with. One young patient had had sex with four partners in one year and got three STDs as a result. From one guy, she contracted gonorrhea. She was without symptoms for an infection that could have caused infertility. The guy confessed later that he had the disease, and she was treated with an antibiotic. Later, another partner shared with her the parasitic trichomoniasis, which caused considerable discomfort and required an unpleasant drug treatment. A third partner bestowed upon her herpes simplex, an incurable viral infection that could necessitate that a future baby be delivered Caesarean section to prevent the infant becoming infected and blinded as a result.

In one case I had to break the news to a fifteen-year-old that she had three STDs at the same time! Am I trying scare tactics here? Yes, because the reality is scary. I would love to herd a bunch of teens who are toying with sex into my office to observe what swollen, blistered, painful herpes look like, or the greenish discharge of gonorrhea. Or perhaps they could witness the painful treatment for burning off genital warts (HPV) that are blossoming all over the vulva. Talk about a reality show!

Fifteen million new cases of STDs are diagnosed each year, and that statistic includes a disproportionate number of sexually active teens. According to the 2002 National Women's Health Report, young women, particularly teens, are more at risk of contracting an STD than any other demographic group.[7] Two-thirds of those who contract an STD are twenty-five or younger and one study found that one in five adolescent girls had an undiagnosed STD.[8] If your daughter is sexually active, her odds are not looking good. Contracting an STD at an early age increases the likelihood for spreading the disease and for possible long-term mental health consequences. In my experience, a girl who has multiple sexual partners is also at risk for depression and troubled relationships with the opposite sex into adulthood. In fact, a 2005 study showed that engaging in sex and drug behaviors places adolescents, and especially girls, at risk for future depression.[9]

Most teens know about the deadly HIV/AIDS virus, which is the STD they are *least* likely to get. But human papillomavirus (HPV)? Chlamydia? Trichomoniasis? Most teens have never heard of these common STDs and don't know how to prevent them or what to do if they contract them. That's why any sexually active girl should have an annual pelvic exam with routine testing for hidden STDs such as HPV and chlamydia, which often have no early symptoms. Any STD has serious long-term health consequences, which can include cervical cancer, infertility, and death. The bacterial and parasitic diseases can usually be successfully treated, but the viral infections, although they can be controlled, are lifelong afflictions.

ALL STDs LISTED CAN BE TRANSMITTED VAGINALLY, ORALLY, AND RECTALLY

HPV (human papillomavirus infection)—viral: May cause genital warts but generally doesn't cause early symptoms. Can lead to cervical, penile, and anal cancer. It causes almost all cases of cervical cancer—6.2 million new cases annually. This is a virus that never goes away.

Trichomoniasis—parasitic: The most common curable STD among young, sexually active women. Most women have an odorous yellow-green discharge and irritation of the vaginal area. Men have slight if any symptoms. Can increase susceptibility for HIV infection and for fallopian tube inflammation—7.2 million new cases annually.

Chlamydia—bacterial: Common STD that can damage reproductive organs. Called the "silent" STD because it typically causes no symptoms. When symptoms occur, they may include vaginal discharge, vague abdominal discomfort, and pelvic pain. Although symptoms are usually mild or absent, serious complications that cause irreversible damage, including infertility, can occur "silently" before a problem becomes apparent. An estimated 2.8 million Americans are infected with chlamydia each year.

Herpes simplex virus—viral: Often no symptoms or minimal symptoms. When symptoms occur, there may be small painful or itchy, red blisters on the vulva, vagina, and cervix that may bleed. Exhibits flu-like symptoms. Open lesions may increase HIV risk. Can infect baby at birth and necessitate a Caesarean section.

Forty-five million U.S. citizens age twelve and above have had genital HSV infection—a virus that never goes away.

Gonorrhea—bacterial: Typically causes no symptoms but may cause thick, puslike discharge, frequent painful urination, and pelvic pain during vaginal penetration. May increase risk of sexually transmitted HIV, pelvic inflammatory disease, and blood infection that causes swollen, painful joints. There are 650,000 new cases annually.

Hepatitis B—viral: Symptoms may not occur at first but include loss of appetite, abdominal discomfort, nausea, and vomiting. In a small percentage of those infected, it may progress to jaundice, liver failure, or liver cancer. The number of new infections per year has declined from an average of 260,000 in the 1980s to about 73,000 in 2003.

Syphilis—bacterial: Symptoms may not appear for years but can include a sore or sores on the external genitals and vagina and in the anus or rectum. Sores can also occur on the lips and mouth. May increase risk of sexual transmission of sexually transmitted HIV, heart disease, blindness, dementia, paralysis, and death. US health officials reported more than 32,000 cases of syphilis in 2002.

HIV/AIDS—viral: Being tested for HIV infection is the only way to know if it is present. Symptoms may not appear for many years. People who are infected with STDs are at least two to five times likelier than uninfected individuals to acquire HIV if exposed to the virus through sexual contact. HIV can lead to AIDS and can result in death.[10]

WHAT DO HORMONES HAVE TO DO WITH SEX?

We have all heard the "raging hormone" excuse for teen misbehavior, and it is important to realize the potency of sex hormones. Seemingly overnight, hormones transform girls into women and boys into men. Actually, it takes a couple of years, but if you study a school portrait of your daughter at age ten side by side with one of her at age thirteen, you'll see the results of potent hormone action. And that is just what you can see!

The hormonal changes during puberty and adolescence are indeed profound, and if the girl is healthy, she is going to become physically able to reproduce in very short order—usually around her twelfth or thirteenth birthday. Although the body is sexually ready in the early teens, the teen brain hasn't caught up. As noted in Chapter 4, current research demonstrates that the decision-making part of the brain doesn't really come into its own until the midtwenties. Teens are ill-equipped in the deepest intellectual sense to fathom the present or future implications of having sex, but the body sure hasn't gotten the message!

If we could separate the thinking part of the brain from the body, we would see that left to its own devices, the sexually mature body wants nothing more than to perpetuate the human race, and there are more or less constant primal urgings in that direction. Sex hormones also have a direct effect on the brain. Inactive areas of the brain are stirred to life by hormones, which stimulate nerve endings and form new connections. These new circuits can create powerful emotions and sexual urges. With the ebb and flow of hormones throughout the menstrual cycle, hormonal changes can trigger some unpleasant symptoms, including moodiness and irritability. But when in balance as nature intended, they can also pave the way for self-assuredness, strength, and energy.

The sex hormones—estrogen, progesterone, and testosterone—don't work in isolation but play in a great endocrine symphony where every note counts. (See Chapter 2 for a more complete description of the hormone action leading to puberty and the continuing menstrual cycle.) Although there are other players, these three hormones are most responsible for the great changes of puberty—and for sexual desire and readiness. Ready or not, when the hormonal symphony starts up, your girl hears music she has never heard before, and she must learn to manage her urges and surges and adapt to her body's incredible changes.

SO WHAT IF SHE'S ALREADY SEXUALLY ACTIVE?

Say you've discovered evidence that she's having sex, vaginal or oral—I'm of the school that considers oral sex *sex*, not abstinence, by the way. You've found birth-control pills or condoms in her room. You overheard a conversation that leaves little doubt. You've discovered a note. You've read her diary. (Not recommended!) Whether shocked or not, you are compelled to *do something*. And well you should. At the least, a teen girl having sex is at risk of humiliation because locker-room boasting hasn't gone away, and the boyfriend of today could be gone tomorrow. At worst, she could contract an STD or become pregnant. It's all bad. The younger she is, the greater danger she faces. So what to do? What to say?

First, gather yourself together and prepare how you will respond. Don't approach her until you're certain you can keep yourself under control. It may help to write down your thoughts and talk over the situation with a trusted family member, preferably her father. Your emotional response may be difficult to handle, especially if her behavior violates the values you have tried to model and instill. I'm not suggesting you ignore your values. But try to get over your anger, because confronting her in anger or guilt tripping her will most likely slam shut the door to communication. If she has had, or continues to have, sexual encounters, you must help her to minimize her risk and to process the changes that being sexually active brings.

Be prepared for her anger and denial. She may tearfully accuse you of snooping or spying on her. She may slam around and throw things. Let it go. This is too important, and your first concern is for her safety. She may also surprise you by being scared and confused, relieved that she no longer has to hide her secret from you, and open to talk. Either way, be calm, be caring, and try to find out:

□ Was this a one-time deal, or is it ongoing?
□ Was a condom used, or is she using birth control?
□ If it was oral sex, was protection used?

- Who is the guy? Is he a classmate, an older student, or worst of all, a twentysomething? Most people assume that when a girl gets pregnant, a classmate is the father, but a Medical Institute for Sexual Health newsletter reported that more than three-quarters of babies born to teen mothers out of wedlock were fathered by men older than twenty. The study also found that men older than twenty father five times more births among junior high school girls than do junior high school boys.[11]

- Were drugs or alcohol involved? A study from the National Center on Addiction and Substance Abuse found that almost one-quarter of sexually active teens and young adults—about 5.6 million fifteen- to twenty-four-year olds annually—report having unprotected sex because they were drinking or using drugs at the time.[12]

- Was the sex consensual or was she coerced? Her answers will provide you with direction. She should be seen by a gynecological provider soon to see if she has contracted an STD, and, if it seems likely that she will continue having sex, that she gets a prescription for contraceptives. This may seem like condoning her actions but it is really just facing reality and providing protection. Remember that if she has unprotected sex, she has a 90 percent chance of getting pregnant during the first year. One of the most tragic ways a teen can become pregnant is when one or both partners believes that being prepared with birth control is wrong because it means that they intended to have sex all along. Christian kids or others who have made an abstinence pledge can be especially prone to this type of thinking. Girls who believe sex is a possibility, but who don't want to take birth-control pills, should carry condoms and insist upon their use should the occasion arise.

WOMAN TO WOMAN

This advice comes from a twenty-four-year-old married woman, whose mother persisted in trying to communicate through her daughter's surly teen moods and rejections. She doesn't know for sure why she was able to resist having sex until she was almost twenty-two years old, but she gives her mother credit for having known something after all.

"Having an open communication line and an open approach to sexuality is so crucial. My mom was always, always, always saying, "If you ever need birth control . . ." She was very upfront about HIV/AIDS and other STDs. She had friends die in the early-mid eighties from AIDS. It was a reality for me. My mom let me know she didn't want me to have sex, but if I did, she wanted me to be safe."

SEX EDUCATION

All parents want their kids to be safe and informed about the possible consequences of sex; we sometimes disagree about how to get there. I believe that comprehensive, age-appropriate abstinence-based sex education is vital in today's sex-charged environment. Abstinence-based sex education courses are the norm today rather than the exception. If your local school isn't teaching abstinence along with anatomy, get involved and instigate change. These courses let kids know that they're not ready for sex, but they do not ignore that many teens are having sex anyway. Teaching about condoms and other forms of protection against pregnancy and STDs doesn't mean the schools are promoting sex. If you are uncomfortable with this, you can ask that she be excused from certain lessons. However, I've seen too many "nice" girls who had unexpected and unprotected sex with dire consequences. My own daughters will get the full program at school as well as values-based abstinence education at home.

WHAT MOMS CAN DO TODAY

1. Let your daughter know from day one that she is unique and wonderful and doesn't need to be like everybody else. If you start in early childhood, and mean it, she may believe it by her teen years and have a greater capacity to withstand peer pressure to dress like a trollop and to have sex.

2. Flip through some magazines and explore with her the ways that young women are used to sell products. Her body and feminine allure give her power and the ability to grab attention. What is she "selling" about herself? Supersexy outfits cause people to make assumptions about her that may not be true.

3. Let her know that even if you don't see her for much of the day, you are watching what she does and that you care. You are on her side, always.

4. Don't assume that she is having sex (vaginal or oral), but also don't assume that she isn't. Keep in mind that over half of teens between ages fifteen and nineteen are sexually active, and it is a sure bet that a lot of their parents are in the dark.

5. Encourage abstinence, but if you discover that she is sexually active, making her safe is your top priority. Make an appointment for her with the family doctor or nurse practitioner. Make sure she has a thorough exam and that she is protected in case her sexual activity continues.

6. Prepare her for her first gynecologic exam. If she is sexually active, her health-care provider will want to perform one to rule out STDs.
7. If she is reluctant to discuss sex with you, leave articles and books around for her to discover.
8. Encourage healthy relationships with peers. Get involved as much as you can and get to know the kids she hangs out with—and their parents too.
9. Support, nurture, be there, and have fun together as a family.
10. Believe that your care, concern, and guidance can make a positive difference in helping her to delay sex.

FOR TEEN EYES ONLY

I know there must be some teen girls who just adore having sex and don't stress about being busted or getting pregnant or contracting an STD or having their college dreams ruined by a failed condom—or by getting dumped by the boyfriend, who then tells everyone who will listen what a stud he is and what he did with or to her. I know there must be some girls, but I have not met any. In fact, I hear just the opposite—sexually active teen girls usually regret losing their virginity and discover that sex is not all its cracked up to be because

□ Many young men are casual or inept regarding condoms, and there can be stress-inducing condom failures, or failure to use one at all.
□ Guys don't have to worry about pregnancy. Many guys care about the girls they're having sex with, but when it comes right down to the wire or the lack of a condom, it's the girl who will carry the baby.

- Guys kiss and tell more freely than girls because it adds to their status, while sharing her sexual exploits tends to diminish hers.
- It's all about him. Sexual pleasure is automatic for guys—if they can get an erection, they can almost always reach orgasm; this is not the case with teen girls. It's not like in the movies.

Here's what some of my teen patients have reported about their "first time."

"Well, after I had sex, my boyfriend rolled over and said that I was pretty good but had a long way to go; this made me feel so terrible. I will never forget that and know I will always think about this if I have sex again."

"It was pretty fun, but it wasn't what I thought it would be, you know, like it is on TV with romance and everything, but I guess it was okay . . ."

"What was I thinking? I could have just shot myself. I would do just about anything to take back that day. It was not worth it, and I knew better."

"I wish I could have saved myself for the man I will marry. My mom told me that I should, and I just didn't believe her, and now I can't change it."

"My first time was pretty bad. I didn't know what to do, and we didn't talk at all. I was embarrassed and felt dirty."

"What is the big deal with sex? Everyone is doing it and makes it out to be some great thing, and it isn't. I could take it or leave it."

"It hurt so bad that I was scared, and I told him to stop, but he was in such a hurry that he didn't."

"The first time I had sex, my boyfriend was nice to me. He helped me through it and was really patient, but the next day at school all the other guys and most of the girls heard about it. I was so mad and embarrassed.

"I don't really like having sex, but my boyfriend tells me he has to have it to relieve the stress and pressure that he has from his home. You know, he has a bad home life."

Emptiness, rejection, frustration, anger, embarrassment, emotional devastation, low self-image, lack of trust, shame, sadness, hurt, despondency, worthlessness, and betrayal. That's what I saw in these girls. I know that it was difficult for them to admit to me that sex really wasn't that great, but I can report that each and every one was profoundly disappointed. As I said before, I know there must be some teen girls who enjoy an active sex life that feels emotionally balanced and about which they have no regrets. *I just haven't met any yet.*

What the Guys Say

I have discussed sex with high school boys over the years while guest lecturing in sex education classes and have asked for their perceptions. What do they think girls get out of sex? How much do they believe girls get involved emotionally? Does sex make them like the girl better? The responses below suggest a disconnect between how teen boys and teen girls perceive sex.

"No way, girls don't care about commitment; they just want to have sex."

"Girls are in it for fun just as much as we are."

"Girls don't get attached like they used to. They are trying to use us as much as we use them."

"I think that girls get attached, but they get over it."

"I know that sex affects girls emotionally, but I don't think it hurts them in any way or stays with them for a long time. They just move on."

A few boys felt that *they* were the ones who had been used and said that when a girl dumped them, they felt rejected, lonely, and embarrassed. Overall, however, the guys' answers displayed a shocking lack of understanding about girls' emotional lives.

I have asked more than fifty high school boys to express their thoughts about virgins. Their responses are revealing.

"I think virgins are cool."

"Virgins are amazing. How do they do it?"

"I have to say, virgins have it goin' on."

"I think virgins have more respect for themselves than girls who are always with guys without even thinking about it."

"Virgins don't really care what guys think."

"Virgins know what they want."

"I'd love to date a virgin."

Not one response revealed anything negative or demeaning about virgins, even though many of these guys said they were themselves sexually active. Don't you find this fascinating?

The bottom line is that nobody wins when teens have sex. It is a rare teen who is emotionally prepared, and girls have more to lose than boys. After all, it is the girl who gets pregnant or faces infertility, cervical cancer, or the prospect of her future child being infected in the birth canal. Our culture has adopted a casual attitude about sex, and young people are paying the price. It is time to share the truth with girls that their sexuality belongs to them and they don't have to give it away.

— 11 —

COMMON COMPLAINTS

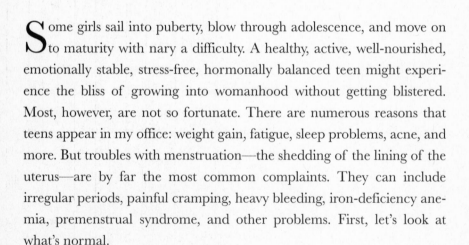

S ome girls sail into puberty, blow through adolescence, and move on to maturity with nary a difficulty. A healthy, active, well-nourished, emotionally stable, stress-free, hormonally balanced teen might experience the bliss of growing into womanhood without getting blistered. Most, however, are not so fortunate. There are numerous reasons that teens appear in my office: weight gain, fatigue, sleep problems, acne, and more. But troubles with menstruation—the shedding of the lining of the uterus—are by far the most common complaints. They can include irregular periods, painful cramping, heavy bleeding, iron-deficiency anemia, premenstrual syndrome, and other problems. First, let's look at what's normal.

FIRST PERIOD

Most women can recall in detail the time and place when they first began to menstruate. Depending upon the education provided by their mothers, sisters, friends, and teachers, they were (1) terrified that they were bleeding to death, (2) elated that they had finally bloomed into womanhood, or (3) saddened that childhood was ending, sensing—correctly—that life would never be the same.

A friend remembers skipping into her home one summer afternoon when she was twelve to cheerfully announce that she had started her period—and wasn't that *great*? She was puzzled when her mother started crying. Years later, with daughters of her own, she understood perfectly. Children, especially some prepubescent girls, can't *wait* to grow up. But mothers know too much about the difficulties that may lie ahead.

Most girls start their periods between ages eleven and thirteen, although the age has been slowly decreasing. The average age of menarche for Caucasian girls is 12.4 and for African-American girls, age 12. There is a wide range of normal. Some girls begin menstruating at nine or ten, others at fifteen or sixteen. As noted in Chapter 2, breasts and pubic hair, signs that puberty has started, may appear in some girls at ages six, seven, eight, or even younger. Girls who experience early puberty generally begin their periods earlier too.

LENGTH OF PERIODS, AND AMOUNT OF FLOW

Menstruation typically lasts three to seven days, and the amount of blood lost ranges from a few teaspoons to about half a cup, with the average between six and eight teaspoons.

TIME BETWEEN CYCLES

By definition, the first day of bleeding is counted as the beginning of each menstrual cycle, or day 1. The cycle ends just as the next menstrual period starts. Cycles range from twenty-four to thirty-four days. Only about 10 to 15 percent of cycles are exactly twenty-eight days long. Generally, the intervals between periods are longest in the years immediately after the period starts and when the reproductive years end with menopause. It is not unusual for a twelve- to fourteen-year-old to have her period once every month and a half, but with the time between periods gradually shortening to between twenty-five and thirty days by her late teens or early twenties. It is also not unusual to skip a month or two during the first couple of years of menstruation.

MINOR DISCOMFORT IS COMMON

Normal physical responses to the menstrual cycle may include some discomfort at the time of ovulation (about two weeks before the period starts), cramping, especially during the first day or two of flow, and edema, irritability, breast tenderness, and weight gain in the week or so before the period. This is later called premenstrual syndrome (PMS), and symptoms can be mild to severe. (See Chapter 9 for more details on this common affliction.) Some girls don't experience it at all. PMS symptoms can be alleviated and, in some cases, prevented.

PERIOD PROBLEMS

Menstruation is supremely dependent upon hormonal signals. Changes in the ovaries lead to the release of estrogen and progesterone at different stages of the cycle. The ovary is under the control of the pituitary gland, which in turn is under the control of the part of the brain called the hypothalamus. Diet, stress, overweight, insulin resistance, thyroid abnormalities, and too little or too much exercise can create disturbances at any point along the chain of command, and menstrual problems can result.

SKIPPING A PERIOD (AMENORRHEA) OR IRREGULAR PERIODS

Outside of pregnancy—the obvious cause for missing a period—there are several reasons why a period can go missing.

1. Age. Hit-and-miss menstruation can persist for up to five years after the first period, but a more-or-less regular cycle is usually established within a couple of years. (Periods and ovulation become irregular again toward the end of the reproductive years.)

2. Exercise. Excessive exercise might cause a skipped period, or even months of skipped periods. Gymnasts, runners, and other athletes who do strenuous daily workouts often experience amenorrhea.

3. Eating disorders and/or extreme weight loss. There is such a thing as being too thin, and most teens with eating disorders are suffering from malnutrition. Malnutrition throws a wrench into hormonal balance, causing all sorts of problems, including disruption of the menstrual cycle.

4. Stress. Stress and highly emotional times may cause a missed period or two, or bring on an early period, more evidence of the profound effects stress can have on the body.

5. Illness. Being sick for a prolonged time can cause the period to take a hiatus or be irregular with light or heavy flow and short or long duration.

6. Polycystic ovary syndrome. See Chapter 8 for details about this condition, which profoundly disrupts hormone balance and may cause periods to cease or to be exceptionally heavy.

7. Problems with the pituitary, thyroid, or adrenal glands. This can lead to hormone imbalance. Undiagnosed thyroid conditions can be behind numerous problems with the menstrual cycle, but the thyroid is often overlooked.

8. Problems with the reproductive organs. This can lead to hormone imbalance.

If the period is skipped for two months in a row, be sure your daughter sees a health-care provider to get to the root of the cause. Not having to put up with a period may seem like a gift from above, but amenorrhea is a health risk. It means there is a lack of circulating estrogens in the body, which can result in premature osteoporosis, impaired performance, infertility, increased risk of injury, and even increased risk of cardio-vascular disease and endometrial cancer.

HEAVY PERIODS

Judging when a period is heavy can be subjective because there is no practical way, short of weighing sanitary pads or tampons before and after use, to precisely measure the menstrual flow. I don't think you want to risk the reaction your daughter might have if you directed her to weigh her tampons or pads before and after use. In addition, the normal range of blood loss is wide—a few teaspoons to a half cup—and the duration of the period may be between three and seven days. If your teen is changing her pad or tampon every hour or so, she is likely experiencing heavier than normal flow.

She may be comforted in knowing that she is not alone. Nearly half of all teens experience at least one heavy period in the first year, and over half of the heavy periods are anovulatory, meaning that the flow is heavy because ovulation did not take place. When ovulation does not occur, progesterone is not available to balance the effects of estrogen. The imbalance, sometimes called estrogen dominance, can cause heavy, crampy periods. It can also cause weight gain, lumpy (fibrocystic) breasts, unstable emotions, irritability, acne, and bloating before the period begins. This combination of symptoms is typical of PMS, the subject of Chapter 9.

Heavy bleeding and failure to ovulate can also result from obesity, eating disorders, and, you guessed it, stress. Other causes of irregular periods include fibroid tumors, which are unusual in women under thirty, and endometriosis, when the lining of the uterus grows outside the womb. Endometriosis most often affects younger women, including teens, before they have children.

Whatever the cause, teens may be frightened by what they think is excessive blood loss and upset by the cramping that often comes with heavy periods. There is little danger if the flow is occasionally heavy and/or the duration of the period is occasionally longer than usual.

Clots are normal too, as the lining of the uterus breaks up. But when excessive blood loss is persistent for two or three months, a health-care provider should be consulted to determine if underlying causes exist. Most often, what seems to be heavy bleeding is within the normal range, but iron-deficiency anemia is a possibility.

ANEMIA

Iron-deficiency anemia is associated with persistently heavy periods. Symptoms include dizziness, pale skin, diarrhea, loss of appetite, abdominal pain, headaches, fatigue, and mental fog. If your daughter has some of these symptoms, and you suspect anemia, simple self-tests can help confirm your suspicion. Push down on her unpolished fingernail bed for two seconds. The area will turn white. Then release and notice how long it takes for the nail bed to turn pink again. If it takes longer than two seconds, low iron or anemia could be the cause. Another test is to pull down the lower eyelid to check the color. If the lower eyelid is pale rather than pinkish red, anemia is a possibility. Feeling winded with exertion and lacking stamina are other common symptoms. Ask your health-care provider for a blood test to measure iron in the blood. Guidelines on treating anemia are listed below.

TREATING ANEMIA

1. **Take iron supplements.** Menstruating teens—many menstruating women, for that matter—need supplemental iron daily, especially if they are vegetarians. Ferrous gluconate, iron gluconate, or iron picolinate are less irritating on the stomach than some iron supplements. I usually prescribe ferrous gluconate in 320 mg doses once or twice daily. The trade name is Fergon, and it is available in tablet or liquid form over the counter. Ferrous gluconate is also available as a generic supplement. Iron supplements should be

taken only if a blood test shows iron deficiency. Excess iron in the blood can be toxic.

2. **Choose foods that are high in iron.** This includes meats, fish, egg yolks, green leafy vegetables, nuts, dried beans and other legumes, and whole grains.

3. **Take vitamin C to enhance iron absorption.** Vitamin C's acidity helps the body absorb the iron from foods and supplements. Squeeze a lemon into a glass of water, eat an orange, or take a 500 mg vitamin C supplement daily.

4. **Cut back on sugar.** Sugar can decrease the body's store of B-complex vitamins and minerals, which can worsen anemia.

5. **Cut back on caffeine.** Found in most sodas, chocolate drinks, coffee, and nonherbal tea, caffeine inhibits iron absorption.

PAINFUL PERIODS—DYSMENORRHEA

At least 50 percent of teens experience painful periods at one time or another, and the worst usually occur during the two or three years following the onset of menstruation. The uterus is primed during each cycle to nourish a fetus, and when a new life doesn't materialize, a buzz of hormonal signals alerts the uterus to jettison its blood-rich lining. Hormonelike substances trigger contractions in the uterine walls, and the resulting discomfort can turn a girl into a miserable, whimpering heap curled into a fetal position. The contractions can cause cramping and sometimes sharp pains in the lower abdomen, lower back, and thighs. The pain starts when the period begins, or shortly before, and lasts for hours, or sometimes as long as a day or two. Nausea and vomiting, diarrhea, sweating, lack of energy, urinary frequency, and depression can be part of this sorry monthly package. A girl may suffer horribly one month and be pain-free the next. Dysmenorrhea gives some credence to those who still call the monthly period "the curse."

Prevention can help. As usual, good nutrition plays a huge part in overall well-being and may help to prevent or ease menstrual cramps. The general guidelines for a healthy diet include eating plenty of fresh fruits and vegetables, whole grains, legumes, eggs, lean meats, fish, and nuts. Avoid commercial junk foods. Sugar, products made from refined flour, and caffeine-loaded sodas are among the worst things a girl can put into her body. The risk of having painful periods increases with

- Use of caffeine or nicotine
- Stress
- Lack of exercise
- Poor nutrition

Note: A girl is also more likely to have serious cramping if her mother had it.

TREATING MENSTRUAL PAIN

In my practice the first line of defense is almost always using herbal or natural remedies. As a society, we have moved away from the tried and true plant-based preparations that have been developed through the centuries. Instead, we opt for quick fixes, such as nonsteroidal anti-inflammatory drugs (NSAIDs), such as aspirin, ibuprofen, or naproxen, some of which can be toxic to the liver, especially if used in excess or with alcohol. NSAIDs work to relieve minor discomfort, but I urge my patients to try natural remedies first.

RELIEVING MENSTRUAL CRAMPS
WITH HERBS AND SUPPLEMENTS

Tori Hudson, a naturopathic practitioner and coauthor of numerous books on natural remedies, suggests using herbs such as black haw, ginger, valerian, and motherwort for menstrual cramps.[1] Valerian is a great relaxant; black haw has been used for centuries to relax the uterus; ginger can relieve nausea; and motherwort has been effective in relieving nearly all gynecological imbalances. Many of my younger patients have found relief by using motherwort alone. Used in a tincture (liquid form), five drops in a glass of water is a good starting point. If cramping is not relieved in ten minutes, another five drops can be taken. Repeat twice daily as long as cramping is a problem. Evening primrose oil also combats the effects of spasm-causing prostaglandins, which trigger uterine contractions.

The supplements recommended below have been studied in clinical trials and have been found to be effective in relieving painful periods. For best results, they should be taken over a three-month period, at the end of which reassessment should occur to monitor improvements and adjust the supplement program accordingly.

MULTIVITAMINS AND MINERALS

A good quality multivitamin and mineral combination forms the foundation of a supplement program. Nutrients known to be helpful for painful periods are then added in small amounts.

□ **Vitamin B$_6$.** Vitamin B$_6$ is needed to help produce "good" prostaglandins, which help to relax and widen blood vessels as opposed to "bad" prostaglandins, which increase uterine contractions and discomfort. This vitamin has been shown to significantly reduce the intensity and duration of period pains.

□ **Vitamin B$_1$.** This B vitamin is effective in easing period pain. In one study, it was given to 556 women (ages twelve to twenty-one years) who had moderate to severe dysmenorrhea. Some of the women were given the B$_1$ first for ninety days and then changed to a placebo. Others were given the placebo first for ninety days and the B$_1$ next. A full 87 percent of the women were completely cured after starting the B$_1$ treatment. This effect remained for at least two months after the B$_1$ was stopped.[2]

□ **Vitamin B$_{12}$.** Because both vitamins B$_1$ and B$_6$ are helpful in treating period pains, the best approach is to take a vitamin B complex. This also provides vitamin B$_{12}$. A combination of fish oil and B$_{12}$ is more effective than fish oil alone for relieving dysmenorrhea.

□ **Vitamin E.** Supplementation of vitamin E may be useful in treating painful periods.

□ **Vitamin C and bioflavonoids.** Vitamin C and bioflavonoids occur naturally together in plants, where they provide a synergistic antioxidant effect. Bioflavonoids are helpful with period pain because they help to relax smooth muscle and reduce inflammation. Bilberry is one of the best bioflavonoids. Others include red grapes and berries of any kind, including blackberries, black currants, and raspberries.

□ **Magnesium.** Magnesium acts as a muscle relaxant, and it has been shown to have a beneficial effect on painful periods and lower back pain. Magnesium, along with vitamin B$_6$, is required to help convert the essential fatty acids into beneficial prostaglandins. Always try to take them together.

□ **Zinc.** This mineral is important for eliminating period pains because it is needed for the proper conversion of essential fatty acids into beneficial prostaglandins.

□ **Essential fatty acids (EFAs).** Taking EFAs in supplement form is extremely important in the treatment of painful periods. Research has shown that women with low intakes of omega-3 fatty acids (the ones that come from fish, flaxseeds, and walnuts) have more painful periods than women who have a high intake. The researchers who found this link also discovered that the extent of the pain was connected to the ratio or balance of the omega-3 and omega-6 fats. The women with the worst period pain ate a much lower ratio of omega-3 fats in relation to omega-6 fats, a 1 to 4 ratio. Omega-6 fats are found in most commercial vegetable oils. I suggest supplementing with fish or flaxseed oil capsules to keep the "bad" prostaglandins under control.[3]

□ **Bromelain.** This is an enzyme contained in pineapples, and it has been found to be extremely useful for treating painful periods. It has anti-inflammatory properties and helps as a natural blood thinner. Bromelain also acts as a smooth muscle relaxant and is thought to decrease the "bad" prostaglandins and increase the "good" prostaglandins.

PAINFUL OVULATION—WHY DOES IT HURT?

Some teens experience discomfort during ovulation, which occurs about midway through the monthly cycle. A German word, *mittelschmerz,* which comes from the German words for "middle" and "pain," is often used to describe the discomfort, which is usually in the middle or side of the abdomen. For some, mittelschmerz really *is* pain, and the discomfort can be severe. For others it is but a twinge. If the pain is severe, nausea can result. Sometimes a small amount of vaginal bleeding or discharge occurs.

During ovulation, the egg and the fluid that surrounds it, as well as some blood, are released from the ovary. It is theorized that the fluid or blood may irritate the lining of the abdominal cavity, causing pain. The pain goes away once the body absorbs the fluid or blood, usually in about twenty-four hours. The same supplements that can help with painful periods may also provide relief for painful ovulation. In difficult cases where the pain is incapacitating and occurs with each ovulation, break out the NSAIDs, such as ibuprofen, which can usually provide relief from this temporary discomfort. As a last resort in severe cases, birth-control pills can be prescribed to stop ovulation.

WHAT IF THE PAIN IS FROM SOMETHING ELSE?

This is where menstrual charting comes in handy. (See p.150.) Ovulation usually occurs about two weeks after the first day of each menstrual cycle, so the timing of the pain makes mittelschmerz easy to recognize. The health-care provider will want to rule out other possible causes of pain, such as an ovarian cyst or endometriosis, where tissue that lines the uterus is growing outside the uterus.

WHEN TO SEE A DOCTOR

Any of the following symptoms during ovulation warrant checking in with a health-care provider.

- ▢ Fever
- ▢ Pain with urination
- ▢ Redness or burning of the skin at the site of the pain
- ▢ Vomiting
- ▢ Midcycle pain lasting longer than a day
- ▢ Spotting between periods that is not associated with ovulation

VAGINAL DISCHARGE

Mucous discharge is normal, and the characteristics and quantity of the discharge vary throughout the month depending upon where a girl is in her menstrual cycle. A clear or whitish vaginal discharge begins about a year before the first period begins. Discharge varies from clear, slippery, and copious, to thick and white. Girls should practice good hygiene, change underpants daily, and not worry about discharge.

However, when discharge is a lot heavier than usual, yellow, foul smelling, or accompanied by itching, a vaginal infection may exist. Some sexually transmitted diseases also cause vaginal discharge. Unusual discharge should be checked out by a health-care provider.

NO DOUCHE!

Teens may want to douche, especially after the period ends or if they are having sex, but douching removes healthy bacteria from the vagina—bacteria that work to protect against infection. Also, the perfumes and scents in douches are irritating. In fact, it is best to avoid using any scented product in the tender genital area.

MENSTRUAL CHARTING

If your daughter is skipping periods, having abdominal pain midway through her cycle, has heavy or painful periods, troublesome PMS, or is experiencing other menstrual symptoms that disrupt her life, it is a good idea to keep track of what is going on cycle by cycle. If she sees a health practitioner because of period problems, the doctor is going to ask for a detailed description of what happens and when, and a menstrual chart can aid in diagnosis. As you know, the first question your provider asks is,

"When was your last period?" Imagine the surprise and delight if your daughter whips out her menstrual chart!

Even if she is not having problems, charting the menstrual cycle is an excellent way for her to get in touch with what is happening in her body. The hormonal ebb and flow will become apparent, and she may even be able to see the effects of stress and the changes wrought by diet and exercise.

You can purchase fancy menstrual charting calendars, download one for free from the Internet, or simply use any calendar expressly for that purpose. It is fun to have one that includes lunar cycles, and many women learn to predict their periods by the phases of the moon. The first day of the period is day 1 in the cycle. During the days of bleeding, note whether the flow is light, heavy, or moderate; whether there is cramping, and whatever other symptoms may occur. In general, the menstrual chart should be a record of anything observable that goes on with the reproductive system.

Ovulation usually occurs about fourteen days after the period begins. You can tell it is coming because vaginal mucus becomes wetter, slippery, or white. On the day of ovulation, mucus is very wet and slippery. It is extremely useful for females of all ages to know that increased mucus signals fertility. The few days before and right after ovulation is the fertility window of the cycle. Ovulation may pass without notice or may cause discomfort. Ovulation-related signs and symptoms should be noted in menstrual charting.

ACNE

To teens, zits are an abomination. If your daughter has an occasional pimple or a smattering of zits at a certain point in her cycle, don't worry. She will survive without physical or emotional scarring, although she will loathe each one. Acne can be another matter. If she has mild to severe acne, she may be profoundly affected. During the years when teens are so incredibly sensitive about looks, constant facial outbreaks are a serious threat to self-esteem and social acceptance. I wish I could recommend a magic remedy to banish acne, but none exists. The best I can do is help with understanding why some girls get it and how best to cope. Fortunately, over-the-counter (OTC) and prescription medications can help to alleviate the condition. Girls should hold on to the truth that they will grow out of it, usually by the late teens.

The male-type hormone testosterone and genetics are to blame for acne. Acne doesn't mean that hormone levels are abnormal, but that some skin types react abnormally to it. The female body starts producing testosterone around the same time that the body begins sprouting hair, about a year before menstruation begins. Testosterone signals glands in the skin called sebaceous glands to produce an oily substance called sebum. Some people's sebaceous glands overreact to testosterone and overproduce oil. To make matters worse, the tiny tubes where sebum is produced get gummy and blocked. Blocked tubes and too much sebum plus normal skin bacteria add up to zits, and lots of them.

Dermatologist Jeri Mendelson, MD, says that some parents seem to think acne results from a combination of too much makeup, bad hygiene, and chocolate, but teens are not to blame.

"Avoiding acne would require changing the family tree," she says. "Diet, hygiene, and make-up may exacerbate acne but they do not impact the overall course. If anything, I see more negative outcomes with the super scrubbers who end up drying out their faces with alcohol-containing products and then suffering rebound effects with more oil production."[4]

So what helps? Dr. Mendelson recommends a topical retinoic acid combined with benzoyl peroxide for mild to moderate cases. For advanced acne, especially if acne has spread to the chest and back, she adds an oral antibiotic, usually minocycline. If there is a cystic component, meaning that the pimples will cause scarring, she may prescribe Accutane.

Some teens find that using an OTC 2.5 percent benzoyl peroxide gel or cream product is effective. A noncommercial Web site, www.acne.org, provides helpful advice. The take-away message: acne can't be cured, but it can be helped.

Before treating, hormone levels should be tested to rule out imbalances that can cause or worsen acne: high testosterone, high estradiol, or low progesterone. Fortunately, these imbalances *can* be treated.

NATURAL REMEDIES FOR ACNE

□ Take vitamin B$_5$. Acne may be stress related. The stress hormone cortisol is produced in excess when stress levels are high. Although the relationship between stress and acne is still being debated, cortisol has been implicated in female acne. Taking pantothenic acid (vitamin B$_5$) can help with fatty acid metabolism, which is underproduced during stress, contributing to acne.

□ Use water-based beauty products, and avoid oil-based products, which may contribute to acne outbreaks.

□ Clean up the diet. Although the correlation between diet and acne is unclear, it makes sense to avoid eating foods that cause inflammation and/or blood sugar instabilities. These would be the usual suspects: refined sugar products and refined grain products. Research has shown that teens with unstable blood sugar levels also have a higher incidence of severe acne.

SLEEP PROBLEMS

Teen girls rarely come to my office specifically because they are having sleep problems, but the results of inadequate sleep become apparent when I take their medical histories. Being chronically sleepy increases stress and affects just about every aspect of life and health. Teens need at least eight and a half hours of sleep every night, and nine hours are better. Why is getting enough sleep so important? Because missing out on an hour or two of sleep every night leads to a sleep deficit over time, which leads to poorer performance in school, athletic endeavors, and situations that require quick reflexes, such as driving. In addition, sleep deficit has been linked to fatigue and emotional troubles such as depression.

According to a 1999 National Sleep Foundation survey, 60 percent of children under the age of eighteen complained of being tired during the day, and teens are more likely to be tired than younger children.[5] Most teens' circadian rhythm, a kind of internal biological clock, is set for getting sleepy after 11:00 p.m. and sleeping until midmorning. This seems to be because melatonin, a hormone that regulates sleeping and waking patterns, is produced later at night for teens than for younger kids and adults.

If your daughter says she is not tired at midnight even though she got up at 6:00 a.m., she is not kidding. But that won't prevent her from having a tough time dragging herself out of bed to get to school on time or staying awake once she gets there. If she has difficulty waking up or a hard time concentrating, and if she falls asleep during classes and feels moody or depressed, she could very well have a sleep deficit.

At the urging of parents and teachers, some middle and high schools have instituted later start times to accommodate teens' biological clocks, and college students attempt to avoid 8:00 a.m. classes. But most school bells ring closer to 7:00 or 8:00 a.m. than to 9:00 or 10:00 a.m., so teens have to figure out how to work adequate sleep into their schedules. Here are some ideas for your sleepy daughter:

□ Avoid caffeine after 4:00 p.m. That includes coffee and tea, of course, but also chocolate and sodas containing caffeine. Nicotine is also a stimulant, and drinking alcohol in the evening can cause a person to have a restless night.
□ In the hour before bedtime, avoid activities that excite the brain such as writing emotional e-mails, playing video games, watching action movies, arguing, or engaging in other stressful activities.
□ Stay away from bright lights, which signal the brain that it's time to

rise and shine. This includes the computer screen.

□ Relax! Before going to bed, dim the lights, play mellow tunes, close your eyes, and try to empty your mind. Taking a warm bath, drinking a cup of herbal tea, and reading can help.

□ Exercise is a great way to stay healthy, and some experts believe working out earlier in the day can help with sleep, but exercising close to bedtime can raise body temperature and keep you awake.

□ Train yourself to go to bed at the same time every night and get up no more than a couple of hours later on weekends than on weekday mornings. This can help to establish sleep patterns and reset your internal clock.

□ Avoid taking naps. If you're sleepy during the day and give in by taking naps, it will be more difficult to fall asleep at night.

□ Plan ahead. If you have a big test or assignment due, avoid staying up into the wee hours the night before. Depriving yourself of sleep the night before a test could have a negative effect on your performance.

SUPPLEMENTS FOR SLEEP

Some compounds can help with getting a good night's sleep. They include:

□ The Sleep Formula (see Appendix A)
□ 5-HTP, 25–50 mg in the evening
□ Calcium/magnesium liquid or capsules, 500 mg/250 mg in the evening (see Appendix A)

FATIGUE

A teen's fatigue can be a result of lack of sleep, of course, but also can be due to other factors, including thyroid problems, autoimmune diseases, poor diet, vitamin deficiencies, stress, lack of exercise, and even chronic fatigue syndrome. If fatigue lasts longer than two weeks and doesn't seem to improve with rest, a visit to a health-care provider is in order.

WHAT MOMS CAN DO TODAY

1. If your daughter hasn't started her period yet, make sure she knows what to expect so that discovering blood in her underpants doesn't scare her.

2. Period problems may be common ground for you and your daughter and a natural way to talk "woman to woman." She will most likely be interested in how you handled menstrual difficulties in your teens. She will also benefit from the information in this chapter regarding what's normal and what's not.

3. Help her get started with menstrual charting. Keep a calendar yourself and compare notes.

4. Once her period has started, switching from a pediatrician to a gynecological provider is a good idea. The American College of Gynecology (ACOG) recommends that teens have their first gynecological visit between ages thirteen and fifteen and their first internal exam and pap by age eighteen.[6] If she isn't sexually active and under age fifteen, the provider probably won't do an internal exam, but now is a good time to prepare her for the inevitable.

5. Talk with your daughter about the importance of getting enough sleep and disciplining herself to keep a regular bedtime. (You can help by enforcing bedtime.) With homework and activities, however, this isn't always possible, but there is value in creating awareness about how much better she will feel and perform if she gets enough rest.

12

TESTING AND TREATING
WITH HORMONES

Hormone imbalances create a wide spectrum of problems for teens. Irregular periods, acne, fatigue, irritability, rage, depression, weight gain, facial hair, insomnia—all can be blamed on out-of-whack hormones. So doesn't it make sense to measure hormone levels to help explain symptoms, identify underlying problems, and accurately prescribe treatment?

Hormone testing is the best way to establish a baseline. While not every teen fits within the normal ranges that are somewhat artificial, testing still provides a guideline from which the hormonal treatment plan is created and tested against in the future. As a result, more and more medical providers are learning how to test and interpret hormone levels so females of all ages can take control of their hormone-related symptoms.

Individuality is the name of the game with testing and treatment. Even though teens may have similar complaints, each has a unique hormone profile and responses to treatment, and a singular lifestyle to which the program must be adapted. Diet, physical activity, and stress levels can affect hormone balance, and these days prescription drugs and environmental hormones are often among the disruptive factors. The possible culprits include asthma medications, steroids, birth-control pills, antidepressants, and hormonelike substances in food additives, household and beauty products, and environmental chemicals. These substances can interfere with the normal cyclic functioning of the ovaries and thus hormone production.

These variables make my job incredibly challenging but also extremely rewarding. I have learned that the one-size-fits-all approach definitely does not apply, and I frequently remind patients that hormone balancing is not a science but an art. This is not instant medicine, but a process. Each patient must be keenly aware of what can cause hormonal disruption and realize that getting into a balanced state can take time. She also must understand that she is not a passive vessel for drugs but an active participant in her own care. The sooner teens, or even preteens, begin taking responsibility for their own health, the better.

The cost of hormone testing is a fraction of the physical, emotional, and financial costs of the hit-and-miss method of discovering which, if any, medications will relieve symptoms. It is also superior to the all-too-common attitude by some in the medical establishment that "female complaints" are somehow imaginary. If someone has already told your daughter that whatever she is experiencing is "all in her head," it probably won't be the last time.

Hormone testing is essential to determine whether your teen would benefit from some type of intervention, including hormones, and it is imperative to test at the correct time during the cycle. If she has regular menstrual cycles, the absolute best time to test is around eighteen days after the first day of her last period or about four to twelve days before she is to begin her next period. It is during this time that the progesterone level is at its peak and circulating levels of estrogen and free testosterone should be most predicable. If you want your daughter to be tested for hormonal balance, ask your medical provider to order a blood/serum panel of estradiol, progesterone, and testosterone one week before the period begins.

SERUM (BLOOD) TESTING

Although some providers favor saliva or urine, I most often prefer serum (blood) testing. While there are occasions when saliva testing is useful, I find that serum testing is of greater value and covered by most insurance companies. Serum testing involves a simple blood draw done in the office or at a lab and is ordered by the medical provider. Serum testing continues to be the worldwide gold standard for evaluating women's hormone levels and is one of the tests routinely used during studies of women's health-care issues conducted by research organizations. Serum tests can be completed by any medical laboratory. Although tests to measure hormone levels have been available for years, it is only recently that they are being done on a regular basis. These tests also have standardized normal values, which makes their interpretation more streamlined. Laboratories have set standards for female hormone levels based on normal cyclic ranges throughout the reproductive years. Serum testing is convenient, timely, accurate, and covered by most insurers. Testing establishes, or rules out, the need for hormone supplementation, and prudent medical providers will order tests before prescribing hormone replacement at any age.

Not all providers are on the same page about testing and treating with hormones, however, and patients who request hormone testing may be told that because levels fluctuate throughout the cycle, testing is not accurate or helpful. If you are fed this line, don't believe it. Hormone researchers use serum testing to identify levels in women before and during treatment, and hormone consultants rely on hormone testing to conduct their evaluations.

The information that has come to light through measuring my patients' hormone levels has been crucial in everything from alleviating PMS to deterring the debilitating effects of chronic fatigue syndrome. It has made the difference in preventing suicide, alleviating excruciating headaches, and curtailing weight gain. In my practice, it would be impossible to do any meaningful work without it.

HORMONES TO TEST

Typically, a teen hormone profile should include information about her levels of estradiol, progesterone, and testosterone. Estradiol is the most potent of the three estrogens, the others being estrone and estriol. Estradiol levels fluctuate throughout the cycle, being highest in the first half of the cycle, falling around the time of ovulation, then rising a bit in the second half of the cycle when progesterone dominates. Testosterone levels appear to have less rise and fall than the other two hormones. If estradiol is not balanced by adequate progesterone during the second half of the cycle, the teen will likely have some (or all!) of the following symptoms:

- Tender, swollen breasts
- Bloating
- Headaches
- Weight gain
- Volatile emotions
- Vaginal yeast infections
- Unstable blood-sugar levels
- Depression
- Irritability
- Water retention

If she fails to ovulate—and most teens have numerous anovulatory cycles in the first couple of years after menstruation begins—her progesterone level will be low during the second half of her period. Low progesterone can result in many of the same symptoms as high estrogen. It is the imbalance between the two hormones that creates most of the symptoms. Symptoms of low progesterone include:

- PMS
- Missed period
- Depression/irritability

□ Breast tenderness

□ Weight gain

□ Dry skin, hair, nails

□ Heavy bleeding and cramping

□ Hair loss

□ Trouble sleeping

□ Less affectionate and/or friendly

Testosterone levels can widely vary in teen girls. If a teen has a high level of testosterone, it could be due to PCOS, diet, genetics, insulin resistance, or adrenal abnormalities. Low testosterone can result from medications such as the birth-control pill or antidepressants.

The effects of high or low testosterone include the following:

High—increased facial hair, irritability, nervousness, hair loss, lack of periods, aggression, acne, weight gain.

Low—fatigue, loss of zest for life, decreased energy, weight gain, loss of strength and endurance, vaginal dryness, and lack of sexual desire.

SERUM (BLOOD) TESTING SPECIFICS

1. The test should be performed seven to ten days before the period or at least eighteen to twenty days after the first day of the last period. For cycles shorter than twenty-eight days, the testing should be done seventeen to twenty days after the first day of the last menstrual period.
2. Serum tests should be interpreted according to what day of the cycle the blood was collected. Days 1 to 14 of the cycle are the follicular phase, and days 15 to 28 are the luteal phase. Knowing when the blood was drawn will determine what the normal ranges are for that specific time of the cycle.

3. When unusually high values occur, but they do not correspond to symptoms, a repeat sample should be requested. Occasionally a false high or low value may occur. It is important that any lab result that doesn't correlate with symptoms, or appears to be markedly off, be repeated for quality assurance.

4. If the value of progesterone is very high on days eighteen to twenty-one of the cycle, indicating that ovulation occurred, but PMS symptoms or other cyclic problems were present at that time, it may be that the abrupt progesterone drop from ovulation until the period begins is causing symptoms. Use of a bioidentical plant-based progesterone the last seven to ten days before the period can correct this problem, even when the progesterone level shows normal in the evaluation.

5. Fasting isn't necessary before blood is drawn to test hormone levels, unless a thyroid panel is ordered for the same time.

6. Teens who are using oral contraceptives, the patch, or a contraceptive ring will need to stop hormone contraception for up to two months prior to testing or the results will be inaccurate. Before stopping, however, a medical provider should be consulted. If the teen is sexually active, the pregnancy risk should be carefully considered.

7. It is generally best to have the levels repeated every three months until balance is achieved, then annually or as needed.

MONTHLY MENSTRUAL CYCLE CHANGES

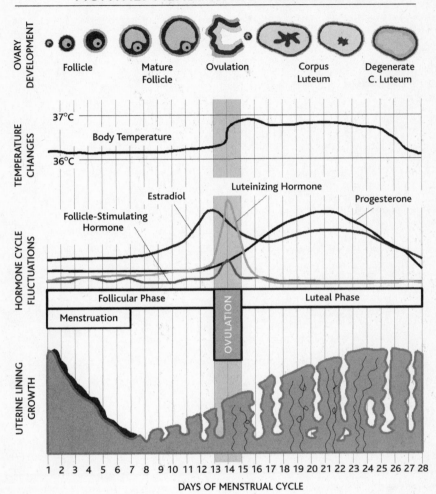

Phases of the cycle:

Secretory Phase	Ovulation Phase	Luteal Phase
Days 1–13	Days 11–15	Days 14–28

*Remember day 1 is always the first day of the period. These ranges are based on an average twenty-eight-day cycle.

NORMAL AND OPTIMAL HORMONE RANGES

Samples taken within three to twelve days before the period.

Estradiol
80–240 pg/ml (normal)
90–200 pg/ml (optimal)

The closer to the period, the lower the number should be, but not below 80.

Progesterone
2.0–17.0 ng/ml (normal)
5.0–17.0 ng/ml (optimal)

The closer to the period, the lower the number should be, but not below 2.0. Levels peak around day 18 of the cycle.

Testosterone
2.2–8.) ng/dl (normal)
3.0–5.0 ng/dl (optimal)

Testosterone remains fairly stable throughout the month; testing should be done in the morning if possible.

The cyclical phases of progesterone and estradiol are shown in the graph above. The rise and fall of estradiol and progesterone follow distinct patterns. As you can see, estradiol peaks around midcycle and progesterone peaks about seven to ten days before the period begins. If testing is done seven to ten days before the period, then the progesterone level should be at least in the midrange of normal. If the progesterone level returns at 1.2 pg/ml, which is below normal, supplementation with progesterone could be helpful. Even if progesterone is measured at 3.0, which is on the low end of normal, and PMS or other hormone-related symptoms are present, using progesterone to raise the level to the mid-range could be beneficial.

ESTROGEN

Estradiol is the most potent of the estrogen hormones, which include estrone and estriol. Together they are essential for the healthy functioning of the reproductive system and for breast development. The estradiol level builds during the first half of the cycle. It fluctuates less in the second half, and levels should decline the closer one gets to the period (see chart on p. 163). If the normal range for estradiol seven to ten days before the period is 80–240 pg/ml, then the closer one gets to the onset of the period, the lower the number should be. If the test was done five days before the period, and the level returned as 200 pg/ml, estrogen dominance would be the diagnosis, and symptoms could include painful breasts, heavy-cramping periods, acne, irritability, and depression. High estradiol levels are nearly always associated with low levels of progesterone, and supplementing with progesterone will bring the ratio of progesterone to estradiol into a more normal range.

PROGESTERONE

Progesterone is produced in the ovaries during the second half of the menstrual cycle. (It is also produced by the placenta during pregnancy.) Small amounts are also produced by the adrenal glands. The progesterone level is low during the first two weeks of the menstrual cycle, peaks at ovulation, approximately day 18 of the cycle, and goes down from there.

TESTOSTERONE

Testosterone levels are more constant and, when measured, should be closer to the midrange of normal. Optimal levels are between 3.0 and 5.0 ng/dl. Teens with testosterone at higher levels are more likely to have acne, weight gain, and excess hair. High testosterone is a strong indicator that a girl has PCOS. (see Chapter 8) Note: Certain medications can lower free testosterone levels in the blood, causing fatigue, hair loss, loss of strength, and reduced mental perfomance.

WORKING WITH YOUR MEDICAL PROVIDER

By the time she is thirteen or fourteen, or earlier if you suspect she is sexually active, your daughter should be seeing a gynecological provider. While pediatricians are proficient in treating diseases and disorders of childhood and adolescence, a gynecological provider will be more attuned to the adult-type female disorders that begin to appear once menstruation begins. The good news is that a growing number of healthcare providers are now familiar with bioidentical hormones and hormone-testing options, and are working with pharmacists who specialize in compounding individualized prescriptions. The bad news is that your provider may not be one of them.

If your medical provider does not know about testing or the use of bioidentical hormones, your best bet is to seek out a provider who does, if only for gynecological care and/or for hormone testing and treatment. To locate a provider near you, contact a compounding pharmacy in your area about obtaining a list of medical providers who are proficient in hormone testing, (see Compounding Pharmacies in Appendix A). If none is available, testing and treating may be done through my Web site, www.hormonesinbalance.com.

While the number of practitioners who recognize the benefits of hormone testing and treatment with bioidentical hormones is growing, it is still news to many. If you would like to have your daughter's hormone levels tested, you have the right to request the exact tests you want along with a copy of the results. Just remember that interpreting test results and ordering the appropriate hormonal treatment is as important as ordering tests in the first place.

CASE STUDY: USING BIOIDENTICAL HORMONES TO TREAT HORMONE PROBLEMS

Becky's mom brought the seventeen-year-old to my office after the family had endured two stressful years of seeking relief for her symptoms. (This is not unusual; patients often search out my practice after other efforts have fallen short.) Becky was struggling. She had serious acne. She continued to gain weight, although she remained physically active in a health-conscious family that was obsessive about exercise. She felt tired, sad, and out of control. Another provider had put her on birth-control pills to bring her heavy periods under control and relieve her acne. While her periods did let up and her acne calmed down a bit, her complexion problems were still troubling, she continued to gain weight, and she felt fatigued and off kilter. In addition, her mother was concerned about the long-term effects of the birth control pills on her daughter's developing body.

CONTRACEPTIVES

Chances are that if a teen shows up in a medical provider's office with acne, heavy, painful periods, mood instability, or any number of other cycle-related complaints, she will end up with a prescription for contraceptives, which include the pill, ring, and patch. However, if the girl does not need a contraceptive to prevent pregnancy, she should avoid taking these powerful synthetic hormones. I prescribe contraceptives for sexually active teens, but I use them only as a last resort for teens who are not sexually active and whose symptoms can generally be brought under control using bioidentical hormones. While the jury is still out on long-term use of synthetic hormones for birth control, they are under investigation for contributing to a number of long-term effects, including breast cancer, blood clots, headaches, depression, and changing insulin needs for diabetics. I believe that we will soon find out that the long-term use of the pill is detrimental.

Hormone-level testing was definitely in order, but Becky had to go off the birth control pills for two months before a hormone profile could be taken; it takes that long for the effects of synthetic hormone medication to disappear. In the meantime, I provided a thorough physical exam, took a detailed medical history (including a rundown of her typical daily diet), and got her started on a healthier eating plan. Becky was in that rare category where her health-conscious family ate well, but she remained a finicky eater heavily drawn to sweets, breads, and processed lunch-meats. She needed to hear from an outside expert—me—that she was doing herself harm with her processed-food diet. Hormone testing two months later revealed that Becky's estrogen and testosterone levels were higher than the normal ranges, and her progesterone level was low. I advised that she stay off the synthetic birth control pills and instead use bioidentical progesterone to be taken daily the two weeks before her period. (She was not sexually active, so birth control was not an issue.) This balanced her high estrogen, and her periods became normal. It took several months, but the combination of progesterone and improved diet finally brightened Becky's health picture. The use of progesterone lowered her free testosterone level without her having to use other medications. Bioidentical progesterone is often enough to bring the other sex hormones into balance. Progesterone is a signaling hormone and a precursor, so it often dictates what other levels are doing or what they should be doing. Now twenty-three, Becky's hormone profile is within normal ranges. She feels good, looks good, and is no longer on progesterone therapy.

BIOIDENTICAL HORMONE THERAPY

I prefer to use bioidentical hormones with my patients. The word *natural* can be confusing. Some of my patients believe that *natural* equates with over-the-counter herbs and vitamins and other nonprescription remedies, and that, as such, they are not as effective as a prescription drug manufactured by a pharmaceutical company. Not true! Bioidentical hormones are powerful and effective. *Bioidentical* means that these hormones have the same molecular structure as your own hormones and function exactly the same way in your body. Bioidenticals are made from soy or wild yam.

My experience with bioidentical hormones versus synthetics is that they provide a more complete correction of symptoms with fewer side effects. In a nutshell, natural hormones, when formulated by a reputable compounding pharmacy,

1. are standardized, FDA-approved substances that can be prescribed for all the same reasons as synthetic hormones;
2. don't have the side effects of synthetics if used properly;
3. can be individualized;
4. won't interfere with the body's own hormone production;
5. match your own hormones molecularly so your body isn't confused by something that almost fits—but not quite;
6. are used more quickly by the body than synthetics and don't pose the same long-term risks.

Progesterone is the most common hormone deficiency I see in teens, due at least in part to the fact that they often have cycles in which ovulation does not occur, and progesterone is largely a product of ovulation. Some would argue that since the first couple of years of menstruation are so unsettled, it is best to wait until a girl has a well-established and predictable menstrual cycle before messing with her hormones. In general, I agree. However, the severity of some girls' symptoms dictates intervention.

Testing is best done the week before the period begins, and although the normal ranges are broad, the treatment goal is to make sure the progesterone level is above 5.0 ng/ml, at its peak (day 21 of the cycle). Some teens need to be on the upper end of normal limits to obtain the optimal effect.

The progesterone replacement that I use in my practice requires a prescription that is formulated according to the individual dose needed.

This is done at a compounding pharmacy, which is a pharmacy whose pharmacists understand how to formulate prescriptions into individualized regimens. In addition to a nonprescription low-dose cream, natural progesterone is available through prescription in many forms:

- Capsules
- Topical gels
- Drops or tablets
- Lozenges
- Vaginal gels/creams
- Suppositories

I have found that sublingual drops and topical creams are effective in increasing blood levels of progesterone and quickly relieving symptoms. For teens, I prescribe it most often on days 14 through 28 of the menstrual cycle, usually starting with the lowest dose, 25 mg, and increasing as necessary.

Here is what to expect when using progesterone:

1. Calmer, more soothing emotions, with less anger, irritability, depression, and abrupt mood swings.
2. Fewer cravings, food binges, blood-sugar lows, and cyclic weight gain.
3. Less bloating, water retention.
4. Improved sleep.
5. More normal periods with less cramping and less bleeding.
6. Better complexion.

GETTING THE MOST FROM PROGESTERONE

If your daughter is taking bioidentical progesterone, help her to monitor her symptoms and progress. Please see the following troubleshooting suggestions, and keep in mind that your medical provider should be consulted with concerns or problems if they develop.

TROUBLESHOOTING GUIDE

1. If your daughter is using progesterone to help get periods back on track or wants lighter periods with fewer cramps, and the desired effect does not occur within two weeks of using the progesterone, this may be a sign to increase the dosage. (The lowest dose is 20 mg.) I suggest raising the dose to at least one-half more during the next cycle. Her medical provider should be consulted first.

2. If spotting occurs before the period is due, she should continue taking the progesterone until the due date for her period and then stop. If heavy bleeding starts when she is taking progesterone, she should stop taking progesterone and count the day the bleeding began as the first day of the new cycle.

3. If her period does not start, she should stop taking the progesterone for two weeks and then resume.

It is always good to keep in mind that treating with hormones is a last resort. It is not a substitute for lifestyle changes that can often alleviate or eliminate symptoms. Lifestyle changes, such as dietary improvement and physical activity, will most likely be necessary even if hormone treatment is pursued. Remember: hormone treatment is part of a holistic plan. It isn't just "take a pill and forget about it." Also, hormone testing is but one tool used in my office. Symptom reporting and monitoring are every bit as important.

If your provider prescribes hormone treatment, it is important to recognize that treating with hormones is a *process* and your daughter is a unique individual who requires a treatment plan that is based on her own profile and symptoms. Adjustments are nearly always necessary during the course of treatment, and patience and mindfulness to her responses are essential for achieving optimal hormonal balance.

Self-treating with herbs, over-the-counter remedies, or nonprescription hormone creams may be helpful, but teens whose symptoms point to hormone imbalance can benefit from testing and evaluation by a medical provider trained in their use. Careful monitoring once treatment is started is as important as arriving at a diagnosis. The relationship among hormones is extremely intricate and complex. Treating with one hormone can and will affect others.

WHAT MOMS CAN DO TODAY

1. If you suspect that your daughter's physical and/or emotional difficulties are hormone related, locate a medical provider who is proficient in hormone testing and treatment and make an appointment. A good way to find a knowledgeable provider is to contact a compounding pharmacy in your area and ask for a list of providers who use their services. (Compounding pharmacies formulate bioidentical hormones and other substances for individual patients.) If you can't find a provider in your locale, visit my Web site, www.hormonesinblance.com.
2. Explore with her the use of herbal remedies and supplements listed in this book for help with specific complaints.
3. If she has been prescribed hormone-balancing medication, help her to monitor her symptoms. Menstrual charting is very useful.
4. Refer your daughter to this book's final chapter for an easy-to-follow, step-by-step plan for hormone balance.
5. Do not give up!

— 13 —

EIGHT STEPS TO HORMONAL HEALTH AND BALANCE

In my office teens with hormone-related problems are thoroughly evaluated and then given a plan based on their specific needs. There are four general areas of focus:

1. Diet and weight
2. Lifestyle and exercise
3. Emotional life
4. Hormone levels

These broad areas are difficult to put into boxes because the mind and body are interdependent, and hormones pretty much run the show on all levels. But we can tease out elements in each area and work on improvements that will affect the whole picture, body and mind. It all works together as we design a program to promote success in the game of balance.

The challenge in working with teens is to keep the program simple. Too often, teens are assigned elaborate programs and/or prescribed medications with multiple side effects that are likely to be tossed aside after only a few frustrating weeks, or even days. A program doesn't have to be that way. By carefully examining all aspects of the teen's life, reviewing potential and existing symptoms, measuring hormone levels, and creating a straightforward plan with close follow-up, a teen can achieve success in eliminating the underlying issues that are causing her grief. A major consideration is that *nobody else can do it for her.* She has to be on board in her own balancing act, and persuading her that feeling and looking great is going to involve effort on her part is essential to success.

Some teens are not even *close* to buying into the program. Exercise to the point of perspiring? Eat five or six servings of fruits and veggies a day? Learn to breathe? Banish bagels and white bread? *Get real, Mom!* The challenge with these girls will be educating them about how much better off they will be if they eat right, exercise, get enough sleep, and learn to handle stress. Others may be tuned in on one area but neglecting the others. Maybe they have the exercise thing down but are still hooked on sodas and Oreo cookies. That won't cut it in the quest for hormone balance. As the mind and body work together, so do the steps outlined below in the quest for hormonal harmony.

These steps distill much of what has been said in previous chapters. Each is important, and all must be addressed if imbalances are to be corrected. No matter where your teen is on the continuum, please don't expect that she will embrace these ideas all at once. You may be discouraged that the recommended dietary and lifestyle changes seem so massive that they will never happen. Perhaps your own habits also need tweaking, and you too need time to adjust to change. But remember that improving one area affects the others, and improvements that occur over months are just as good as those that happen overnight. It is all a process that can be taken one step at a time.

STEP 1. IMPROVE THE DIET

Food is the number one medicine. Period. It is also the number one poison. Everything that goes into the mouth affects the body on a cellular level, and diet has a major impact on physical, mental, emotional, and hormonal balance. Unfortunately, I meet few teens during a first visit to my office who have their diets under control. Here are the how-to-eat basics:

- Eat a hearty breakfast that includes protein, good fat, and fiber. A good breakfast improves focus, decreases fatigue, and blasts food cravings. Research has shown that people who eat a good breakfast eat less throughout the day and tend to lose weight. A few choices: half a grapefruit, oatmeal, and hard-boiled eggs; sprouted grain toast with peanut butter and a small apple; one of the new high-protein, high-fiber cereals with blueberries, milk, and/or slow cooked oatmeal.

- Banish sugar. Except for an occasional treat, sugar should *not* be part of the daily diet. Sugars produce insulin/blood sugar highs and lows, lead to food cravings, and add calories without even a trace of nutritive value. Read labels to locate hidden sugars in processed foods. Naturally occurring sugars, such as those in whole fruits, are a healthier way to satisfy a sweet tooth. Use stevia, xylitol, or agave for sweetening, if needed.

- Eat whole grains including old-fashioned oats, brown and wild rice, and breads and pastas made from whole grains. Sprouted grain bread products are best. Teens who are trying to lose weight should strictly limit grains of any kind.

- Get rid of junk food. This is a given if you have accomplished the above. Stop tempting your teen with sugary treats stashed around the house. This includes sodas, fruit juices, processed crackers, chips, sugary cereals, and candy. No one needs this stuff.

- Eat healthy fats. Unrefined oils are best. Extra-virgin olive oil, sesame oil, avocados, nuts, seeds, coconut oil, and butter are among the "good" fats. Fats to avoid include most vegetable oils (soybean, corn, cottonseed, etc.) and the trans fats that are present in most packaged bakery goods, margarines, and restaurant frying oils. If the words "partially hydrogenated" are on the packaging label, avoid the product.

□ Eat whole fruits and vegetables, five to eight servings daily.

□ Drink more water. Try to get your daughter to drink a full glass with breakfast, take a water bottle to school and finish it every day, and then drink two or three more glasses after school and before bed. Tell her that her complexion will shine with more water.

□ Eat three meals a day and a couple of healthy snacks in between to keep metabolism stoked. Tell her that she will burn more fat if she eats when she gets hungry.

□ Get the entire family on board with this way of eating; you all will feel and look better.

STEP 2. ACHIEVE AND MAINTAIN
A HEALTHY WEIGHT

If weight is an issue with your daughter, as it is with many teens, follow the advice above with these caveats:

□ Limit grains. Although they are nutritious, most whole grain products are also high in carbohydrates. Eating fewer bread-based or flour-based foods will reduce the appetite, curtail cravings, and lead to weight loss without the pain of working against a ferocious appetite. See Appendix A for various detailed diet plans.

□ Choose berries such as raspberries, strawberries, blueberries, and blackberries over more typical fruits such as apples, oranges, and bananas. Berries have lower sugar content and more fiber than most fruits. Avoid sweet tropical fruits such as mangoes and pineapples.

□ Eat mostly dark green vegetables such as broccoli, spinach, kale, and lettuces. Avoid starchy vegetables, especially potatoes. Cauliflower is a good potato substitute.

◻ Although I don't recommend counting calories, it is important to be realistic about portion sizes. If your daughter still feels hungry after a meal, waiting twenty minutes will often solve the problem. Drinking water also helps.

◻ Exercise is critical to weight loss. Aerobic exercise burns calories, and strength training builds muscles. More muscle means a zippier metabolism, which means the body burns more stored fat.

STEP 3. SUPPLEMENT THE DIET

Starting your teen on supplements will save her from many illnesses and hormonal disruptions. If she is like me and doesn't want to swallow umpteen pills, she could do as I do and use Energy Infusion Powder, which comes in orange and berry flavors. Just one scoop in water provides more than forty vitamins, minerals, antioxidants, and amino acids that are essential to whole-body balance. The basic supplement plan for a teen should include:

◻ High-potency B complex after breakfast
◻ Daily multivitamin
◻ Calcium-magnesium—500 mg/200 mg in the evening
◻ Fish oil capsules—1000 mg daily, or flaxseed oil capsules, flax oil, or ground flax seeds, 1 TBSP daily

STEP 4. EXERCISE, EXERCISE, EXERCISE!

Although exercise doesn't have its own chapter in this book, it is frequently mentioned and is integral to achieving hormonal balance. Aerobic exercise, such as walking, jogging, dancing, or cycling; and anaerobic, such as weight lifting and resistance training, are equally important. Aim for at least thirty minutes of daily exercise. If your daughter wants to invite a friend over, tell her that if she goes for a twenty-minute walk with you or her friend, you will allow the extra "friend time."

STEP 5. DE-STRESS YOUR TEEN'S LIFE

You may not be able to control the outside world and the pressure exerted by peers, school, and the craziness of our hectic culture, but you can control what goes on in your own home. Help to reduce your teen's stress load, and your own at the same time, by practicing the following.

☐ Practice positive talk, thinking, and actions. Use good, healthy words when speaking in person or on the phone. Stay away from nagging, comparing, beating up verbally, or judging. Practice the kind of talk you want spoken to you. Fill your home with positive talk, looks, gestures, and reinforcement. You will get back what you give out!

☐ Breathe, breathe, and breathe! Teach your daughter to slow down and be aware of breathing in and breathing out, slowly, mindfully. Deep, conscious breathing, as opposed to quick shallow gulps, fuels her cells and helps her to be more alert and energetic. Encourage her to breathe before or during tests, sports or music performances, after a confrontation, or under other stressful circumstances. It will be something that will help her, her entire life. Practice breathing together: breathe in to the count of six, holding for three counts, and then releasing to the count of eight. Ahhhh. Done before bed, this will also help her get to sleep quickly.

☐ If she is overbooked, as most teens are, help her to prioritize and drop things from her schedule.

☐ Teach her to cook at home, and get into the calming exercise of preparing wholesome food together.

☐ Encourage her with your positive attitude. Instead of nagging, "Jill . . . come on! We are *late*," say, "Jill, how can I help you get to school on time? Is there something I can do for you?" Pulling the "late, hurry-up" pressure talk during your limited time together will dampen your relationship with her and send her off for the day stressed from the get-go.

□ Pray with your daughter, if she is open to this, and consider having tea, going to lunch once a week, or providing a way to de-stress. This is difficult because, as a mother, your life is full also. But you only get one chance at this opportunity, and what you teach your daughter will stay with her for life!

STEP 6. SHE'S NO BABY,
BUT SHE SHOULD SLEEP LIKE ONE

Sleep is the repair shop of the body, and we must think of it as such for our daughters and ourselves. Getting to sleep late and getting up early, and consistently getting less than the recommended number of hours of sleep—eight and a half to nine and a half hours for teens—contributes to hormonal havoc.

□ Help your teen to eliminate late-night preparations for the next morning, especially last-minute studying. No starting the report due the next day at 9:00 p.m. or 10:00 p.m.! Help her to plan her week and head off these late deadlines!

□ Eliminate computer use, video games, and watching action-type movies within an hour of bedtime. All stimulate the release of cortisol, tricking the brain into thinking it is time for action, not rest. Also, the emotional state that e-mailing often creates can interfere with sound sleep.

□ Encourage baths, chamomile tea, lavender on the pillow, shoulder and neck massage, and other calming exercises that promote relaxation before bedtime.

□ Studies still show that getting a minimum of eight hours is what is needed for the average adult. With teens it most likely is nine hours or more. When you add physical, mental, or emotional stress to the picture, the night repair sleep time increases.

STEP 7. PRACTICE MOOD MANAGEMENT

If your teen is often depressed, anxious, angry, or irritable, please don't consider it normal. We all have our moments, but foul moods and/or depression day after day, week after week, are unhealthy and unnecessary. Don't let time slip away without making sure she is on the right track for balance in this important area. Whether through the simple measures listed below or by enlisting the services of a professional, she can be helped.

- ☐ Immediately improve her diet to get her blood sugar under control. This act alone helps to smooth out nearly 70 percent of the mood disorders that I see in the office.
- ☐ Sleep deprivation contributes to mood disorders. She needs eight and a half to nine and a half hours of sleep every night. Help her to achieve this.
- ☐ Add mood-boosting supplements such as 5-HTP, 25–50 mg nightly. This can be increased to 100 mg if necessary. This supplement can be used while taking an antidepressant, but only under the supervision of a medical provider who is knowledgeable about amino acids. Also, a high potency B-complex supplement will help her mood by supporting the neuro-brain chemicals necessary for optimal balance.
- ☐ If she continues to struggle with depression, anxiety, or irritability after trying the measures listed above, consider having her tested for neuro-chemical imbalances. See www.neurorelief.com for details.
- ☐ Eye movement desensitization and reprocessing specialists can provide significant support and relief from trauma, negative energy, and depression. My favorite specialist is Richard Ross. I highly recommend Richard and his "Life Transformation" work. You can find out more about his unique sessions and his products geared toward teen balance at www.richardross.com.

□ Teach positive talk. Ask your daughter and a girlfriend or two to journal every thought they have about themselves for one day. That evening, maybe over dinner, ask the girls to share their thoughts. Make it a plan to reverse their negative thoughts and begin talking and thinking healthily. They must learn that they will become who they think they are.

STEP 8. CONSIDER HORMONE ANALYSIS

Before you ask your medical provider to order hormone testing, make sure that you have applied the principles listed in steps 1–7 above. If after three months of improved diet, adequate sleep, sufficient exercise, and stress-relieving measures your teen still has emotional or physical problems related to her menstrual cycle, it may be time to measure blood levels of estrogens, progesterone, and testosterone.

□ Have the hormones tested in the second half of the cycle, at least eighteen days from the first day of the last period. Ask for a serum estradiol, progesterone, free testosterone, thyroid levels, ferreting, and CBC levels.

□ Have your medical provider review the results with you. If the provider is not up to date with the most recent information on hormone balancing and testing, consult our service at www.hormonesinbalance.com for a personal consult.

□ Once a treatment plan has been started, have the hormone levels retested in three months to assure that the treatment is working.

Putting the Eight Steps to Hormonal Health and Balance into practice with your teen should be fun. No kidding! The physical and mental improvements that will result will blow her away, and you too. Keep education at the front of this program. Read some of the books listed in Appendix A. Pass them along to your teen and others in the family, and don't leave out her friends. Everyone can learn from these steps.

Your teen has but one shot at growing up healthy and happy. As her mom, you have the power to manage and/or influence so many important elements of these tender yet tough years. Please use your love and care to put into motion the principles of achieving the hormonal balance that can result in her excellent mental and physical health. I wish you and your daughter well on your journey!

NOTES

CHAPTER 1

1. Shankar Vedantam, "Children's Use of Antidepressants Soars," *Washington Post*, April 19, 2004. http://www.ahrp.org/infomail/04/04/19a.php.
2. Shankar Vedantam, "Psychiatric Drugs' Use Drops for Children: Suicide Warnings Raise Bigger Fears on Testing Process," *Washington Post*, October 8, 2005. http://www.ahrp.org/infomail/05/10/08.php.
3. National Institutes of Health, "U.S. Teens More Overweight Than Youth in 14 Other Countries," *NIH News*, January 5, 2004. http://www.nih.gov/news/pr/jan2004/nichd05.htm.
4. Council on Families, "Marriage in America: A Report to the Nation," 1995. ChildTrends DataBank. www.americanvalues.org/html/r-marriage_in_america.html.

CHAPTER 2

1. Natalie Angier, *Woman: An Intimate Geography* (Boston: Houghton Mifflin, 1999), 185.
2. Herman-Giddens, et al., "Secondary Sexual Characteristics and Menses in Young Girls Seen in Office Practice: A Study from the Pediatric Research in Office Settings Network," *Pediatrics* 99 (April 1997) 502-12.
3. Paul Kaplowitz, MD, PhD, *Early Puberty in Girls* (New York: Ballantine, 2004), 75.

CHAPTER 3

1. Centers for Disease Control as reported in Health Policy Notes archive, March 22, 2005, http://www.do-online.osteotech.org/blog/index.php?catid=17&blogid=4&archive=2005-032.
2. Learn more about compounding pharmacies in Appendix A.

CHAPTER 4

1. The Impact of Mental Illness on Society, a National Institutes of Mental Health fact sheet, 2001. http://www.nih.gov/publicat/burden.cfm. The fact sheet describes data developed by the Global Burden of Disease study conducted by the World Health Organization, the World Bank, and Harvard University.
2. American Academy of Child and Adolescent Psychiatry. Teen Suicide, updated July 2004. http://www.aacap.org/publications/factsfam/suicide.htm.
3. United States Department of Health and Human Services. The Surgeon General's Call to Action to Prevent Suicide, 1999. http://www.surgeongeneral.gov/library/calltoaction/fact3.htm.
4. National Youth Violence Prevention Resource Center, Teen Suicide. http://www.safeyouth.org/scripts/teens/suicide.asp.

5. Centers for Disease Control and Prevention, "Youth Risk Behavior Surveillance—United States, 1999," CDC Surveillance Summaries, June 9, 2000, *MMRW* 2000; 49 (No. SS-5), 10.
6. Elizabeth Wurtzel, *Prozac Nation, Young and Depressed in America: A Memoir* (New York: Penguin, 1994), 21.
7. "FDA Launches a Multi-pronged Strategy to Strengthen Safeguards for Children Treated with Antidepressant Medications," *FDA News*, October 15, 2004. http://www.fda.gov/bbs/topics/news/2004/NEW01124.html.
8. Julia Ross, M.A., interview February 10, 2005.
9. Commission on Children at Risk, *Hardwired to Connect: The New Scientific Case for Authoritative Communities* (New York: Institute for American Values, 2003).
10. National Institute of Mental Health, *Teenage Brain—A Work in Progress* (Bethesda, MD: U.S. Department of Health and Human Services, 2000), www.nimh.nih.gov.
11. National Institute of Mental Health, *Depression in Children and Adolescents. A Fact Sheet for Physicians* (Bethesda, MD: U.S. Department of Health and Human Services, 2000), www.nimh.nih.gov.
12. Gregory N. Clarke, PhD, et al., "A Randomized Trial of a Group Cognitive Intervention for Preventing Depression in Adolescent Offspring of Depressed Parents," *Archives of General Psychiatry*, December 12, 2001, 58: 1127-34.
13. Julia Ross, MA, interview February 10, 2005.

CHAPTER 5
1. National Institutes of Health, "U.S. Teens More Overweight Than Youth in 14 Other Countries," *NIH News*, January 5, 2004, http://www.nih.gov/news/pr/jan2004/nichd05.htm.
2. "Preventing Diabetes and Its Complications," Centers for Disease Control and Prevention, Chronic Disease Prevention, www.cdc.gov/nccdphp/publications/fact-sheets/Prevention/diabetes.htm.
3. Stephen Cook, MD, et al., "Prevalence of a Metabolic Syndrome Phenotype in Adolescents: Findings from the Third National Health and Nutrition Examination Survey, 1988-1994," *Archives of Pediatrics and Adolescent Medicine* (August 2003) 157: 821-27.
4. Richard F. Heller and Rachael F. Heller, *Carbohydrate Addicted Kids: Help Your Child or Teen Break Free of Junk Food and Sugar Cravings—for Life!* (New York: HarperPerennial, 1998), 47.
5. Kelly D. Brownell, PhD, "Fast Food and Obesity in Children," *Pediatrics* (January 24, 2004), http://pediatrics.aappublications.org/cgi/content/full/113/1/132.

CHAPTER 6
1. Mary Enig, PhD., and Sally Fallon, *Eat Fat, Lose Fat* (New York: Hudson Street Press, 2005).
2. Ibid., 47-48.
3. Harvard School of Public Health, "Carbohydrates: Carbohydrates and the Glycemic Index," http://www.hsph.harvard.edu/nutritionsource/carbohydrates.html.
4. CSPI's Guide to Food Additives. http://www.cspinet.org/reports/chemcuisine.htm.

5. Michael F. Jacobson, PhD, "Liquid Candy Supplement, Softdrink Consumption 1999-2002" (Center for Science in the Public Interest, June 2005), www.cspinet.org/liquidcandy/. Accessed June 26, 2006.

6. Christian B. Allan, PhD, and Wolfgang Lutz, MD, *Life Without Bread: How a Low-Carbohydrate Diet Can Save Your Life* (Los Angeles: Keats Publishing, 2000), 151.

CHAPTER 7

1. Julia Ross, MA. *The Diet Cure* (New York: Penguin, 1999), 33.

2. National Eating Disorders Association, Eating Disorders Information Index, http://www.edap.org/p.asp?WebPage_ID=294.

CHAPTER 10

1. Peter Bearman, PhD, and Hannah Bruckner, PhD. "After the Promise: The STD Consequences of Adolescent Virginity Pledges," *Journal of Adolescent Health* 36 (April 2005): 271-78.

2. Robert E. Rector, "The Effectiveness of Abstinence Education Programs in Reducing Sexual Activity Among Youth," Backgrounder #1533, Heritage Foundation, www.heritage.org/Research/Family/BG1533.cfm.

3. The National Campaign to Prevent Teen Pregnancy, "One in Five Have Sex Before Their 15th Birthday: New Report Details the Sexual Behavior of Young Adolescents," May 20, 2003, (news release).

4. Alan Guttmacher Institute, "Teenagers' Sexual and Reproductive Health: Developed Countries," www.agi-usa.org/pubs/fb_teens.html.

5. Neil Osterwell, "Oral Sex is Common Among Teens to Prevent STDs and Pregnancy," *Medpage Today.* http://www.medpagetoday.com/OBGYN/STDs/tb /1754. Accessed June 26, 2006.

6. Lisa Remez, "Oral Sex Among Adolescents: Is It Sex, or Is It Abstinence?" *Family Planning Perspectives* 32, no. 6 (November-December 2000), agi-usa.org/pubs/journals13229800.html.

7. "Sexually Transmitted Diseases and Women's Health," National Women's Health Report, June 2002. www.findarticles.com/p/articles/mi_m0NKT/is_3_24/ai_97185464.

8. H. Wiesenfeld, D. Lowry, R. Heine, et. al., "Self Collection of Vaginal Swabs for the Detection of Chlamydia, Gonorrhea, and Trichomoniasis: Opportunity to Encourage Sexually Transmitted Disease Testing among Adolescents," *Sexually Transmitted Diseases* 28, no. 6 (June 2001): 321-25.

9. Denise D. Hallifors, et al., "Which Come First in Adolescence—Sex and Drugs or Depression?" *American Journal of Preventive Medicine* (October 2005), www.cpc.unc.edu/uploads/4823/1764/which_first_final.pdf. Accessed June 26, 2006.

10. Sexually Transmitted Diseases. STD Topics. U.S. Center for Disease Control and Prevention, http://www.cdc.gov/std/, and American Social Health Association.

11. The Medical Institute for Sexual Health. The Medical Institute Advisory Weekly E Newsletter, http://www.medinstitute.org/health/questions_answers.html#listitem17667460. Accessed June 26, 2006.

12. Underage Drinking Fact Sheet, *Time* 159, no. 13 (April 1, 2002), http://www.oasas.state.ny.us/prevention/OASAS_TOOLKIT/resources/Information_sheets/toolkit_factsheet.pdf. Accessed June 26, 2006.

CHAPTER 11

1. Tori Hudson, *Women's Encyclopedia of Natural Medicine* (Lincolnwood, IL: Keats, 1999), 181.

2. G.E. Abraham, "Nutritional Factors in the Etiology of the Premenstrual Tension Syndromes," *The Journal of Reproductive Medicine* 28, no. 7 (1983): 446-64.

3. F. M. Harel, Biro, R. K. Kottenhahn, and S. L. Rosenthal, "Supplementation with Omega-3 Fatty Acids in the Management of Dysmenorrhea in Adolescents," *American Journal of Obstetrics and Gynecology* 174 (1996)

4. Jeri Mendelson, MD, personal interview, November 6, 2005.

5. National Sleep Foundation, "Poll Shows U.S. Children Complain of Daytime Sleepiness, Fall Asleep at School," 1999, www.sleepfoundation.org/hottopics/index.php?secid.

6. American College of Obstetricians and Gynocologists, "ACOG Clarifies Recommendations on Cervical Cancer Screening in Adolescents," September 30, 2004, www.acog.org/from_home/publications/press_releases/nr09-30-04-1.cfm.

SOURCE MATERIALS

CHAPTER 1

Teens Today

Bradlow, H. L., D. L. Davis, G. Lin, D. Sepkovic, and R. Tiwari. "Effects of Pesticides on the Ratio of 16 Alpha/2-Hytroxyestrone: A Biological Marker of Breast Cancer Risk." *Environmental Health Perspectives* 103, no. 7 (October 1995): 147–50.

Fagan, Patrick F., and Kirk A. Johnson, Ph.D. *Marriage: The Safest Place for Women and Children*. The Heritage Foundation Backgrounder 1535, April 10, 2002.

Hall, D. "Nutritional Influences of Estrogen Metabolism." *Applied Nutritional Science Reports*, 2–4.

Kaplowitz, Paul, M.D., Ph.D. *Early Puberty in Girls: The Essential Guide to Coping with This Common Problem*. New York: Ballantine, 2004.

"Marriage in America: A Report to the Nation." Council on Families, 1995. ChildTrends DataBank.

Shankar, Vedantam. "Children's Use of Antidepressants Soars." *Washington Post*, April 19, 2004.

CHAPTER 2

The Teen Hormone Takeover

Aeby, Tod C., M.D. "Dysfunctional Uterine Bleeding." EMedicine, Instant Access to the Minds of Medicine. http://www.emedicine.com/PED/topic628.htm.

Bacon, George E., et al. *A Practical Approach to Pediatric Endocrinology*. Chicago: Year Book Medical Publishers, 1982.

Lemonick, Michael D. "Teens Before Their Time." *Time*, October 30, 2000.

Neinstein, L. S., and F. R. Kaufman. "Normal Physical Growth and Development," chap. 1 in *Adolescent Health Care: A Practical Guide*. 4th ed. Philadelphia: Lipincott, Williams & Wilkins, 2002.

Richards, Byron J. *Mastering Leptin: The Leptin Diet, Solving Obesity and Preventing Disease*, 2nd ed. Minneapolis: Wellness Resources Books, 2004.

Rogan, Walter J., and Beth Rogan. "Evidence of Effects of Environmental Chemicals on the Endocrine System in Children." *Pediatrics*, July 2003.

CHAPTER 3

Stressed Out

Beisel, W. R., and M. I. Rapport. "Inter-relations Between Adrenocortical Functions and Infectious Illness." *New England Journal of Medicine* 280, no. 11 (March 13, 1969): 596–604.

Callies, F., M. Fassnacht, et al. "Dehydroepiandrosterone Replacement in Women with Adrenal Insufficiency: Effects on Body Composition, Serum Leptin, Bone Turnover, and Exercise Capacity." *Journal of Clinical Endocrinology and Metabolism* 86, no. 5 (May 2001): 1968–72.

Garver, Lloyd. "When All A's Isn't Good Enough." Opinion by Lloyd Garver. *Modern Times*. CFSNews.com. April 9, 2003.

Jefferies, W. M. "Cortisol and Immunity." *Medical Hypotheses* 34, no. 3 (March 1991): 198–208.

Weinhouse, Beth. "De-Stressing Family Life." *Child*, October 2003.

White, K. S., and A. D. Farrell. "Anxiety and Psychosocial Stress as Predictors of Headache and Abdominal Pain in Urban Early Adolescence." *Journal of Pediatric Psychology*, 2005.

CHAPTER 4

The Teen Mood Mountain

American Association of Suicidology Youth Suicide fact sheet, www.suicidology.org.

Bond, A. J., J. Wingrove, and D. G. Critchow. "Tryptophan Depletion Increases Aggression in Women During the Premenstrual Phase." *Psychopharmacology* 156, no. 4 (August 2001): 477–80.

The Brown University Child and Adolescent Behavior Letter 18, no. 4 (April 2002).

Byerley, W., L. Judd, F. Reimherr, and B. Grosser, "5-Hydroxytryptophan: A Review of Its Antidepressant Efficacy and Adverse Effects." *Journal of Clinical Psychopharmacology* 7 (1987): 127–37.

Child and Adolescent Violence Research at the National Institutes of Mental Health, 2000. http://www.nimh.nih.gov/publicat/violenceresfact.cfm.

Clarke, Gregory N., Ph.D. "Cognitive-Behavioral Treatment of Adolescent Depression: Efficacy of Acute Group Treatment and Booster Sessions." *Journal of the American Academy of Child & Adolescent Psychiatry* 38, no. 3 (March 1999): 272–79.

Clarke, Gregory N., Ph.D., et al. "A Randomized Trial of a Group Cognitive Intervention for Preventing Depression in Adolescent Offspring of Depressed Parents." *Archives of General Psychiatry*, December 12, 2001.

Das, Y. T., M. Bagchi, D. Bagchi, and H. G. Preuss. "Safety of 5-Hydroxy-l-Tryptophan," *Toxicology Letter* 150, no. 1 (April 2004): 111–22.

Depression Learning Path, http://www.clinical-depression.co.uk/Depression_Information/teen.htm.

Farkes, Dunner, and Fieve, "L-Tryptophan in Depression," *Biological Psychiatry*, 1976.

"FDA Launches a Multi-Pronged Strategy to Strengthen Safeguards for Children Treated with Antidepressant Medications." *FDA News*, October 15, 2004. http://www.fda.gov/bbs/topics/news/2004/NEW01124.html.

Focus Adolescent Services. *Teen Depression: Warning Signs, Information, Getting Help.* www.focusas.com/Depression.html.

Glenmullen, Joseph, M.D. *Prozac Backlash: Overcoming the Dangers of Prozac, Zoloft, Paxil, and Other Antidepressants with Safe, Effective Alternatives.* New York: Touchstone, 2000.

Goode, Erica. "Stronger Warning Urged on Antidepressants for Teenagers." *New York Times*, February 3, 2004.

Greenburg, Gary. "Is It Prozac or Placebo?" *Mother Jones*, November–December 2003.

Hardwired to Connect: The New Scientific Case for Authoritative Communities. New York: Institute for American Values.

Jones, B. J., and T. P. Blackburn. "The Medical Benefit of 5-HT Research." *Pharmacological Biochemistry and Behavior* 71, no. 4 (April 2002): 555–68.

Kishimoto, H., Y. Hama, T. Nagasaki, and M. Konno. "Plasma Amino Acid Concentrations in Depressed Patients." *Yokohama Medical Bulletin*, 1978.

Maurizi, C. P. "The Therapeutic Potential for Tryptophan and Melatonin." *Medical Hypotheses* 31 (1990): 233–42.

Murray, M. *5-HTP* (New York: Bantam Books, 1998).

National Mental Health Association fact sheet: Adolescent Depression—Helping Depressed Teens. http://www.nmha.org/infoctr/factsheets/24.cfm.

Persson, T., and B. Roos. "5-Hydroxytryptophan for Depression." *Lancet* 2 (1967): 987.

Poeldinger, W., et al. "Functional Dimensional Approach to Depression." *Psychopathology* 24 (1991): 53–81.

Robertson, J., and T. Monte, *Natural Prozac* (San Francisco: Harper, 1997).

Rohr, U. D. "The Impact of Testosterone Imbalance on Depression and Women's Health." *Maturitas* 41, no. 1 (April 2002): 25–46.

Sandyk, R. "L-Tryptophan in Neuro Psychiatric Disorders: A Review." *International Journal of Neuroscience* 67 (1992): 24–144.

Schloss, P., and D. C. Williams. "The Serotonin Transporter: A Primary Target for Antidepressant Drugs." *Journal of Psychopharmacology* 12, no. 2 (1998): 115-21.

Takahashi, S., H. Kondo, and N. Kato. "Effect of L-5-Hydroxytryptophan on Brain Monoamine Metabolism and Evaluation of Its Clinical Effect in Depressed Patients." *Journal of Psychiatric Research* 12, no. 3 (1975): 177–87.

Van Praag, H. M. "In Search of the Action of Antidepressants, 5HTP, Tyrosine Mixtures in Depression." *Neuropharmacology* 22 (1983): 433–40.

Van Praag, H. M., and R. Kahn, "L-5-Hydroxytryptophan in Depression and Anxiety." *Schweizerische Rundschau für Medizin* 77 (1988): 40–46.

Van Praag, H. M., et al. "Therapeutic Indications for Serotonin Potentiating Compounds, a Hypothesis." *Biological Psychiatry* 22 (1987): 205–12.

Young, S. N., and K. L. Teff, "Tryptophan Availability, 5HTP Synthesis and 5HT Function." *Progress in Neuro-psychopharmacology and Biological Psychiatry* 13 (1989): 373–79.

CHAPTER 5

Stopping the Fat Train

Aude, Y. W., P. Mego, and J. L. Mehta. "Metabolic Syndrome: Dietary Interventions." *Current Opinions in Cardiology* 19 (2004): 473–79.

"Carbohydrates. Going with the (Whole) Grain." *Harvard School of Public Health Nutrition Source.* www.hsph.harvard.edu/nutritionsource/carbohydrates.html.

Carroll, S., and M. Dudfield. "What Is the Relationship Between Exercise and Metabolic Abnormalities? A Review of the Metabolic Syndrome." *Sports Medicine* 34 (2004): 371–418.

Case, C. C., P. H. Jones, and K. Nelson, et al. "Impact of Weight Loss on the Metabolic Syndrome," *Diabetes Obesity Metabolism* 4 (2002): 407–14.

Cook, Stephen, M.D., et al. "Prevalence of a Metabolic Syndrome Phenotype in Adolescents: Findings from the Third National Health and Nutrition Examination Survey, 1988–1994," *Archives of Pediatrics and Adolescent Medicine*, August 2003.

Flier, J. S., C. R. Kahn, and J. Roth. "Receptors, Antireceptor Antibodies and Mechanisms of Insulin Resistance," *New England Journal of Medicine* 300, no. 8 (February 1979): 413–9.

Heller, Richard F., and Rachael F. Heller. *Carbohydrate Addicted Kids: Help Your Child or Teen Break Free of Junk Food and Sugar Cravings—for Life!* (New York: HarperPerennial, 1998).

Manson, J., P. Skerrett, et al. "The Escalation Pandemics of Obesity and Sedentary Lifestyle," *Archives of Internal Medicine* 164 (2004): 249–58.

Ogden, C. L., C. D. Fryar, M. D. Carroll, and K. M. Flegal. "Mean Body Weight, Height, and Body Mass Index, United States 1960-2002," *Advance Data from Vital and Health Statistics*, no. 347. National Center of Health Statistics, Centers for Disease Control and Prevention, 2004.

Pate, R., M. Pratt, S. Blair, et al. "Physical Activity and Public Health; a Recommendation from the Centers for Disease Control and Prevention and the American College of Sports Medicine." *JAMA* 273 (1995): 402–7.

"Preventing Childhood Obesity: Health in the Balance." Press release. September 30, 2004. Institute of Medicine, www.iom.edu.

"Preventing Diabetes and Its Complications." Centers for Disease Control and Prevention, Chronic Disease Prevention. www.cdc.gov/nccdphp/publications/fact-sheets/Prevention/diabetes.htm.

Schlosser, Eric. *Fast Food Nation.* (New York: Perennial, 2002).

Steinbaum, S. R. "The Metabolic Syndrome; An Emerging Health Epidemic in Women," *Progressive Cardiovascular Disease* 46 (2004): 321–36.

"Sweet Facts You Should Know about Sugar." http://www.askdrsears.com/html/4/T045000.asp.

"U.S. Teens More Overweight Than Youth in 14 Other Countries." *NIH News,* January 5, 2004. www.nichd.nih.gov/new/releases/teen_obesity.cfm.

Wurtman, J. "Carbohydrate Craving, Mood Changes, and Obesity." *Journal of Clinical Psychiatry*, supplement 49 (1988): 37–39.

Yoo, S., T. Nicklas, and T. Baranowski, et al. "Comparison of Dietary Intakes Associated with Metabolic Syndrome Risk Factors in Young Adults: The Bogalusa Heart Study." *American Journal of Nutrition* 80 (2004): 841–48.

CHAPTER 6

Eating for Life

Appleton, Nancy, Ph.D. "146 Reasons Why Sugar Is Ruining Your Health." www.rheumatic.org/sugar.htm.

Bliss, Rosalie Marion. "Survey Links Fast Food, Poor Nutrition Among U.S. Children." January 5, 2004. USDA Agricultural Research Service. www.ars.usda.gov/is/pr/2004/040105.htm.

Bonvie, Bill, and Linda Bonvie, "A Game of Hide and Seek—Hidden MSG in Processed Foods." *Vegetarian Times*, September 1998.

Esposito, K., R. Marfella, M. Ciotola, et al. "Effect of a Mediterranean-Style Diet on Endothelial Dysfunction and Markers of Vascular Inflammation in the Metabolic Syndrome: A Randomized Trial." *JAMA* 292 (2004): 1440–46.

The Glycemic Index, University of Sydney. www.glycemicindex.com.

Kall, M. A., O. Wang, and J. Clausen, "Effects of Dietary Broccoli on Human in Vivo Drug Metabolizing Enzymes: Evaluation of Caffeine, Oestrone and Chlorzoxazone Metabolism." *Carcinogenesis* 17, no. 4 (April 1996): 793–99.

Metcalfe, Edl, Betty Martini, and Mark Gold. "Sweet Talking—Research Shows Potential Health Risks of Aspartame." *The Ecologist*, June 2000.

Mindell, Earl, and Hester Mundis. "How to Avoid Common Toxins in Your Food." *Natural Health*, May–June 2003.

Neumark-Sztainer, et al., "Adolescent Vegetarians: A Behavioral Profile of a School-Based Population in Minnesota." *Archives of Pediatrics & Adolescent Medicine*, August 1997.

Rizkalla, S. W., L. Taghrid, M. Laromiguiere, et al. "Improved Plasma Glucose Control, Whole-Body Glucose Utilization, and Lipid Profile on a Low-Glycemic Diet in Type 2 Diabetic Men: A Randomized Controlled Trial." *Diabetes Care* 27 (2004): 1866–72.

Wright, J. "Cabbages, Broccoli, et al. Versus Sex Hormone Related Cancers." *Nutrition and Healing* 7 (February 2000): 1–8.

Wu, T., E. Giovannucci, T. Pischon, et al. "Fructose, Glycemic Load, and Quantity and Quality of Carbohydrate in Relation to Plasma C-Peptide Concentrations in US Women." *American Journal of Clinical Nutrition* 80 (2004): 1043–49.

CHAPTER 7

Eating Disorders

Kaplan-Seidenfeld, Marjorie. E., M.D., and Vaughn I. Rickert, Psy.D. "Impact of Anorexia, Bulimia and Obesity on the Gynecologic Health of Adolescents." *American Family Physician*, August 2001.

Meguid, M. M., S. O. Fetissov, M. Varma, T. Sato, L. Zhang, A. Laviano, and F. Rossi-Fanelli. "Hypothalamic Dopamine and Serotonin in the Regulation of Food Intake." *Nutrition* 71, no. 6 (June 2000): 1421–32.

National Institute of Mental Health. "The Numbers Count: Mental Disorders in America; A Summary of Statistics Describing the Prevalence of Mental Disorders in America." Revised 2006.

CHAPTER 8

PCOS—A New Epidemic?

Apridonidze, T., P. A. Essah, M. J. Iuorno, and J. E. Nestler. "Prevalence and Characteristics of the Metabolic Syndrome in Women with Polycystic Ovary Syndrome." *Journal of Clinical Endocrinology and Metabolism* 90 (2005): 1929–35.

Barclay, L. "New Guidelines for Polycystic Ovary Syndrome." *Fertility Sterility* 81 (2004): 19–25.

Cussons, A., B. Stuckey, J. Walsh, V. Burke, and R. Norman. "Polycystic Ovarian Syndrome: Marked Differences Between Endocrinologists and Gynecologists in Diagnosis and Management." *Clinical Endocrinology* 62 (2005): 289–95.

Ehrmann, D., and D. Rychlik. "Pharmacologic Treatment of Polycystic Ovary Syndrome." *Seminars in Reproductive Medicine* 21 (2003): 277–83.

Goldman, Erik L. "Modest Weight Loss Goes Far in PCOS Patients—Better Endocrine, Reproductive Function." *OB/GYN News*, March 1, 2003.

Jancin, Bruce. "Metformin Appears Effective in Teens with PCOS." *Family Practice News*, August 15, 2000.

Kahsar-Miller, C. Nixon, and L. R. Boots. "Prevalence of Polycystic Ovary Syndrome (PCOS) in First-Degree Relatives of Patients with PCOS." *Fertility Sterility* 75 (2001): 53–58.

Kumar, A., K. S. Woods, A. Bartolucci, and R. Azziz. "Prevalence of Adrenal Androgen Excess in Patients with the Polycystic Ovary Syndrome (PCOS)." *Clinical Endocrinology* 62 (2005): 644–49.

Pannill, M. "Polycystic Ovary Syndrome: An Overview." *Nursing eJournal* 2 (2002).

Tsilchorozidou, T., C. Overton, and G. Conway. "The Pathophysiology of Polycystic Ovary Syndrome." *Clinical Endocrinology* 60 (2004): 1–17.

CHAPTER 9

PMS—Pretty Mean Stuff

Ahlgrimm, M. "Managing PMS and Perimenopause Symptoms." *Advanced Nurse Practitioner* 11 (May 2003): 53–54, 90.

Anim-Nyame, N., C. Domoney, N. Panay, J. Jones, J. Alaghband-Zadeh, and J. W. Studd. "Plasma Leptin Concentrations Are Increased in Women with Premenstrual Syndrome." *Human Reproduction* 15 (November 2000): 2329–32.

Dalton, Katherine. *Once a Month: Understanding and Treating PMS.* 6th ed. Alameda, CA: Hunter House,

Domoney, C. L., A. Vashisht, and J. W. Studd. "Use of Complementary Therapies by Women Attending a Specialist Premenstrual Syndrome Clinic." *Gynecological Endocrinology* 17 (February 2003): 13–18.

Frye, G. M., and S. D. Silverman. "Is It Premenstrual Syndrome?" *Postgraduate Medicine* 107 (2000): 5.

Mancho, P., and Q. T. Edwards. "Chaste Tree for Premenstrual Syndrome." *Advance for Nurse Practitioners* (May 2005): 43–46.

Pöldinger, W., B. Calanchini, and W. Schwarz. "A Functional-Dimensional Approach to Depression: Serotonin Deficiency as a Target Syndrome in a Comparison of 5-Hydroxytryptophan and Fluvoxamine." *Psychopathology* 24 (1991): 53–81.

Rasgon, N., M. Serra, G. Biggio, M.G. Pisu, L. Fairbanks, S. Tanavoli, and A. Rapkin. "Neuroactive Steroid-Serotonergic Interaction: Responses to an Intravenous L-Tryptophan Challenge in Women with Premenstrual Syndrome." *European Journal of Endocrinology* 145 (July 2001): 25–33.

Wuttke, W., H. Jarry, V. Christoffel, et al. "Chaste Tree (Vitex Agnus Castus): Pharmacology and Clinical Indications." *Phytomedicine* 4 (2003): 348–57.

Wyatt, K. M., P. W. Dimmock, M. Frischer, P. W. Jones, and S. P. O'Brien. "Presribing Patterns in Premenstrual Syndrome." *BMC Women's Health* 19 (June 2002): 4.

CHAPTER 10

Sex—Teens Don't Have to Give It Away

Jones, R. K., J. E. Darroch, and S. Singh. "Religious Differentials in the Sexual and Reproductive Behaviors of Young Women in the United States." *Journal of Adolescent Health*, April 2005.

"National Longitudinal Study of Adolescent Health." *Surveys Measuring Well-Being.* September 14, 2000. http://www.wws.princeton.edu/~kling/surveys/AddHealth.html.

Rector, Robert E. "The Effectiveness of Abstinence Education Programs in Reducing Sexual Activity Among Youth." Backgrounder #1533 Heritage Foundation. www.heritage.org/Research/Family/BG1533.cfm.

CHAPTER 11

Common Complaints

Dalton, Katherine. *Once a Month: Understanding and Treating PMS*. 6th ed. Alameda, CA: Hunter House.

Mendelson, Jeri, M.D. Personal interview. November 6, 2005.

CHAPTER 12

Hormone Testing and Treating

Arem, R., and D. Escalante. "Subclinical Hypothyroidism: Epidemiology, Diagnosis, and Significance." *Advanced Internal Medicine* 41 (1996): 213–50.

Change, Lee, Linares-Cruz, and Lignieres Fournier. "Influences of Percutaneous Administration of Estradiol and Progesterone on Human Breast Epithelial Cell Cycle in Vivo." Study presentation at Reproductive Endocrinology. Portland, OR, 2004.

De Lignieres, B. "Oral Micronized Progesterone." *Clinical Therapeutics* 21 (January 1999): 41–60.

Fitzpatrick, L. A., and A. Good. "Micronized Progesterone: Clinical Indications and Comparison with Current Treatments." *Fertility Sterility* 72 (September 1999): 389–97.

Martorano, J. T., M. Ahlgrimm, and T. Colbert. "Differentiating Between Natural Progesterone and Synthetic Progestins: Clinical Implications for Premenstrual Syndrome and Perimenopause Management." *Comprehensive Therapeutics* 24 (June–July 1998): 336–9.

Rohr, U. D. "The Impact of Testosterone Imbalance on Depression and Women's Health." *Maturitas* 41, no. 1 (April 2002): 25–46.

Walker, C. R. "Bioidentical Hormone Replacement Therapy. A Natural Option for Perimenopause and Beyond." *Advanced Nurse Practitioner* 9 (May 2001): 39–42, 45.

Wartofsky, L. "The Scope and Impact of Thyroid Disease." *Clinical Chemistry* 42 (January 1996): 121–4.

APPENDIX A

RESOURCES AND SUPPORT

COMMON COMPLAINTS
Once a Month: Understanding and Treating PMS, Katharina Dalton and Wendy Holton.
The Acne Cure: The Revolutionary Nonprescription Treatment Plan That Cures Even the Most Severe Acne and Shows Dramatic Results in as Little as 24 Hours, Terry J. Dubrow and Brenda D. Adderly.
www.acne.org. A noncommercial site providing detailed take-it-from-somebody-who-has-been-there advice on treating acne with OTC remedies.
www.sleepfoundation.org. All you need to know about sleep, including a section on teens and sleep.

DEPRESSION
Change Your Brain; Change Your Life, Daniel Amen.
Foods and Mood, Elizabeth Somer, M.A., R.D.
The Mood Cure, Julia Ross, M.A.
Overcoming Teen Depression: A Guide for Parents, Miriam Kaufman, M.D.
Invisible Girls: The Truth About Sexual Abuse—A Book for Teen Girls, Young Women, and Everyone Who Cares About Them, Patti Feuereisen.
Prozac Backlash: Overcoming the Dangers of Prozac, Zoloft, Paxil, and Other Antidepressants with Safe, Effective Alternatives, Joseph Glenmullen, M.D.
Prozac Nation, Young and Depressed in America: A Memoir, Elizabeth Wurtzel.
www.parentsmedguide.org. Practical advice on antidepressants endorsed by more than a dozen national organizations.
www.aacap.org. American Academy of Child and Adolescent Psychiatry.
www.healthyplace.com. Forum, chat rooms, case studies, and comprehensive information about depression. (Click on the depression community link.)
www.about.com. Teen depression treatment options, hope and direction for parents of depressed teens, diagnosing teen depression, statistics.
http://www.kidshealth.org. For parents and health-care providers.
http://www.braincenter.org/teenage-brain-development.html. Information on teen brain development.
www.richardross.com. Offers consultations on emotional healing and emotional freedom.

DIET AND WEIGHT
Super-Size Me. One guy's experiment with eating nothing but McDonald's food for thirty days.
Syndrome X: The Complete Nutritional Program to Prevent and Reverse Insulin Resistance, Jack Challem, Burton Berkson, and Melissa Diana Smith.
The Insulin Resistance Diet: How to Turn off Your Body's Fat-Making Machine, Cheryle Hart, M.D.

Fast Food Nation: The Dark Side of the All-American Meal, Eric Schlosser.

Sugar Blues, William Duffy. The 1975 classic that linked sugar consumption to nearly every human malady.

The Diet Cure: 8-Step Program to Rebalance Your Body Chemistry and End Food Cravings, Weight Problems, and Mood Swings—Now, Julia Ross, M.A.

Life Without Bread: How a Low-Carbohydrate Diet Can Save Your Life, Christian B. Allan, Ph.D., and Wolfgang Lutz, M.D.

Mastering Leptin: The Leptin Diet, Solving Obesity and Preventing Disease, 2nd ed., Byron Richards.

Excitotoxins: The Taste That Kills, Russell L. Blaylock, M.D.

Carbohydrate-Addicted Kids, Help Your Child or Teen Break Free of Junk Food and Sugar Cravings—for Life! Drs. Richard F. Heller and Rachel F. Heller.

Living the Low Carb Life: From Atkins to The Zone, Choosing the Diet That's Right for You, Jonny Bowden, M.S., C.N.S.

The Ultimate Weight Solution for Teens, Jay McGraw.

Understanding Childhood Obesity, J. Clinton Smith.

Slim and Fit Kids: Raising Healthy Children in a Fast Food World, Judy Mazel and John Monaco.

Get the Sugar Out, Ann Louise Gittleman.

Eat Fat, Lose Fat, Mary Enig, Ph.D., and Sally Fallon.

http://www.cspinet.org/reports/chemcuisine.htm. List of food additives rating their safety. Includes numerous warnings and degrees of caution.

www.rheumatic.org/sugar.htm. "146 Reasons Why Sugar Is Ruining Your Health," Nancy Appleton, Ph.D.

www.glycemicindex.com. University of Sydney's extensive source for classifying foods according to the speed at which the body converts carbohydrates to glucose.

www.MayoClinic.com. BMI calculator for kids.

http://www.parentteen.com/teens_eating_healthy.html. Eating patterns, eating disorders, and tips for the teen diet.

http://www.cdc.gov/growthcharts. Growth charts for children and teens.

EATING DISORDERS

Body Image, Eating Disorders, and Obesity in Youth: Assessment, Prevention, and Treatment, Kevin Thompson and Linda Smolak.

The Diet Cure: The 8-Step Program to Rebalance Your Body Chemistry and End Food Cravings, Weight Problems, and Mood Swings—Now, Julia Ross, M.A.

Preventing Eating Disorders among Pre-Teen Girls: A Step-by-Step Guide, Beverly Neu Menassa.

"I'm Like, So Fat!" Helping Your Teen Make Healthy Choices About Eating and Exercise in a Weight-Obsessed World, Dianne Neumark-Sztainer.

Over It: A Teen's Guide to Getting Beyond Obsession with Food and Weight, Carol Emery Normandi.

www.anred.com. Anorexia Nervosa and Related Eating Disorders, Inc.

www.anad.org. National Association of Anorexia Nervosa and Associated Disorders.

www.nationaleatingdisorders.org. National Eating Disorders Association.

www.nowfoundation.org. National Organization for Women's "Love Your Body Campaign."

www.4woman.gov. National Women's Health Information Center.

http://www.edauk.com. Information and help on all aspects of eating disorders.

800-931-2237. National Eating Disorders Association confidential helpline.

FITNESS
Fitness Training for Girls: A Teen Girl's Guide to Resistance Training, Cardiovascular Conditioning and Nutrition, Katrina Gaede.
Fit Kids: The Complete Shape-Up Program from Birth Through High School, Kenneth Cooper, M.D.
Toning for Teens: The 20-Minute Workout That Makes You Look Good and Feel Great! Joyce Vedral.

HORMONES
The Hormone Connection: Revolutionary Discoveries Linking Hormones and Women's Health Problems, Gail Maleskey and Mary Kittel.
ABC's of Hormones, Jack Challam.
Hormonal Balance: Understanding Hormones, Weight, and Your Metabolism, Scott Isaacs.
Early Puberty in Girls: The Essential Guide to Coping with This Common Problem, Paul Kaplowitz, M.D., Ph.D.
The Hormone Solution: Naturally Alleviate Symptoms of Hormone Imbalance from Adolescence Through Menopause, Erika Schwartz.
Woman: An Intimate Biography, Natalie Angier.
The Hormone Survival Guide for Perimenopause: How to Balance Your Hormones Naturally, Nisha Jackson.
http://www.aap.org/family/puberty.htm. Information on physical changes in teen girls.

POLYCYSTIC OVARY SYNDROME
Androgen Disorders in Women: The Most Neglected Hormone Problem, Theresa Cheung.
PCOS Diet Book: How You Can Use the Nutritional Approach to Deal with Polycystic Ovary Syndrome, Collette Harris.
What to Do When the Doctor Says It's PCOS: (Polycystic Ovarian Syndrome), Milton Hammerly and Cheryl Kimball.

SEX AND ABSTINENCE
Teen Virtue: Real Issues, Real Life . . . A Teen Girl's Survival Guide, Vicki Courtney.
The Truth About Sex by High School Senior Girls, Kristen Anderson.
Great Love for Girls: Truth for Teens in Today's Sexy Culture, Chandra Peele.
What's a Girl to Do? While Waiting for Mr. Right, Janet Folger.
"Sex and Your Teen: What Parents and Health Care Professionals Should Know," Pamela Peeke, M.D.
National Women's Health Report, June 2002.
Adolescent Wellness and Reproductive Education (AWARE) Foundation, http://www.awarefoundation.org, 215-955-9847. Offers reproductive health education materials for teens, parents, and educators.

STRESS
The Cortisol Connection: Why Stress Makes You Fat and Ruins Your Health and What You Can Do About It, Shawn Talbott, Ph.D.
Adrenal Fatigue: The 21st Century Stress Syndrome: What It Is and How You Can Recover, James Wilson N.D., D.C., Ph.D.
Healing the Hardware of the Soul: How Making the Brain-Soul Connection Can Optimize Your Life, Love, and Spiritual Growth, Daniel Amen.

The Relaxation Response, updated and expanded edition, Herbert Benson.
Secrets of the Teenage Brain, Sheryl Feinstein.
Emotional Intelligence, Daniel Coleman.
Dealing with the Stuff that Makes Life Tough: The 10 Things That Stress Teen Girls Out and How to Cope with Them, Jill Zimmerman Rutledge.
Helping Children Manage Stress: A Guide for Adults, James Humphrey.
Stress-Proofing Your Child, Sheldon and Sheila Lewis.
KidStress: What It Is, How It Feels, How to Help, Georgia Witkin.
www.adrenalfatigue.org. Helpful to those who experience persistent or severe emotional or physical stress.

For Teens
Be True to Yourself: A Daily Guide for Teenage Girls, Shannon Berning.
Teen Virtue: Real Issues, Real Life . . . A Teen Girl's Survival Guide, Vicki Courtney.
For Teens Only; Quotes, Notes, and Advice You Can Use, Carol Weston.
Girls Who Rocked the World, Michelle Roehm.
Girls Think of Everything: Stories of Ingenious Inventions by Women, Catherine Thimmesh.
Getting to Know the Real You: 50 Fun Quizzes Just for Girls, Harriet S. Mosatche, Ph.D.
Girls: What's So Bad About Being Good? How to Have Fun, Survive the Preteen Years, and Remain True to Yourself, Harriet S. Mosatche, Ph.D.
Chicken Soup for the Christian Teenage Soul: Stories to Open the Hearts of Christian Teens, Jack Canfield.
Girlwise: How to Be Confident, Capable, Cool and in Control, Julia Devillers.
The Diet for Teenagers Only, Barbara Schroeder and Carrie Wiatt.
Nobody's Perfect: Stories by Teens About Body Image, Self-Acceptance, and the Search for Identity, Kimberly Kirberger
www.health.org/gpower. Girl Power! U.S. Department of Health and Human Services site encouraging girls ages nine to thirteen to make the most of their lives.
http://www.girlscircle.com/index.htm. Organization helping teen girls hold on to their voices and stay true to themselves.

For Parents
Don't Stop Loving Me: A Reassuring Guide for Mothers of Adolescent Daughters, Ann F. Caron.
Healthy Child, Whole Child: Integrating the Best of Conventional and Alternative Medicine to Keep Your Kids Healthy, Stuart Ditchek M.D.
How to Say It to Teens, Richard Heyman, Ed.D.
The O'Reilly Factor for Kids: A Survival Guide for America's Families, Bill O'Reilly.
Between Two Worlds: The Inner Lives of Children of Divorce, Elizabeth Marquardt.
"I'm Like, So Fat!" Helping Your Teen Make Healthy Choices About Eating and Exercise in a Weight-Obsessed World, Dianne Neumark-Sztainer.
You're Wearing That? Understanding Mothers and Daughters in Conversation, Deborah Tanner.
Reviving Ophelia: Saving the Selves of Adolescent Girls, Mary Pipher, Ph.D.
http://www.keepkidshealthy.com. Comprehensive pediatricians' guide to children's health and safety.
http://www.parentteen.com. A look at the joys and challenges facing parents with teens.

COMPOUNDING PHARMACIES

For products such as progesterone cream, please call (888) 99V-WELL or go to www.ventanawellness.com. This resource can also direct you to a compounding pharmacy near you.

Hormones in Balance Program, designed by Nisha Jackson
www.hormonesinbalance.com
(888) 998-9355
Aimed at detecting underlying hormone imbalance and providing testing and consultation for treatment.

For general information about compounding pharmacies and locating one near you contact:
International Academy of Compounding Pharmacists (IACP)
www.iacprx.org
(800) 927-4227

Professional Compounding Centers of America, Inc. (PCCA)
www.pccarx.com
(800) 331-2498

You may also contact any of these compounding pharmacies directly for information and referrals:
Ventana Compounding
www.ventanawellness.com
(888) 99V-WELL

Women's International Pharmacy
www.womensinternational.com
(800) 279-5708

College Pharmacy
www.collegepharmacy.com
(800) 888-9358

MedQuest Pharmacy
www.mqrx.com
(888) 222-8956

HORMONE TESTING LABORATORIES AND SERVICES

Rogue Clinical Laboratories
Testing service for Ventana Wellness
www.rogueclinicallaboratories.com
(888) 998-9355

AAL Reference Laboratories
www/antibodyassay.com
(800) 552-2611

Vitamin Testing:
SpectraCell Laboratories, Inc.
www.spectracell.com
(800) 227-5227
Testing to measure specific macronutrients or vitamins.

HORMONES IN BALANCE
Consultation for hormone imbalances. Includes phone consultation, testing, and follow-up for appropriate treatment, guidelines and recommendations for balance.
www.hormonesinbalance.com
1-888-99V8-9355

NeuroScience Inc.
www.neurorelief.com
(888) 342-7272
Research-driven company specializing in measuring natural chemicals called brain neurotransmitters and recommending natural treatment for such problems as insomnia, depression, ADD/ADHD, autism, fatigue, migraine headaches, and anxiety.

PRODUCT SOURCES
All supplements listed in this book are available from the following reputable suppliers.
Amazon Herb Company
www.rainforestbio.com
(800) 835-0850
This company specializes in products that enhance the effects of natural hormones or are used in place of hormones.

Hahnemann's Laboratories
www.hahnemannlabs.com
(888) 427-6422
This laboratory has combination homeopathic remedies for specific hormonal symptoms.

Rx Vitamins
www.rxvitamines.com
(800) 792-2222
Distributed through medical providers.

Ventana Wellness, PC
www.ventanawellness.com
(888) 99V-WELL (998-9355).
My Web site to help women identify supplements for different life stages and for specific hormonal problems. Free consultations on supplements are available. Testing for nutritional deficiencies or food allergies is also available.

www.vitaminexpress.com
(415) 564-8160
This Bay Area vitamin resource offers a full spectrum of mail order health foods and vitamins.

Western Research Laboratories
(877) 797-7997
www.westernresearchlaboratories.com
A resource for natural thyroid products.

Sprouted and/or Whole Grain Products
Look in your grocery's health food section, in refrigerated area, or freezer for products by The Alvardo Street Bakery, Food for Life, the Silver Hills Bakery, La Tortilla Factory, Tumaro's Gourmet Tortillas, or others made from sprouted whole grains. These products are typically low in carbohydrates but high in fiber and protein.

Recommended Protein Bars
Peak Protein Bars, www.peakbars.com
Power Protein Bars
Met-Rx Protein Bars
Zone Bars
Balance Bars
Promax Bars

PRODUCTS BY NISHA

Information on all of the products listed here can be obtained through www.ventana wellness.com or by calling (888) 99V-WELL (998-9355).

Teen Daily Supplement
Provides essential vitamins, minerals, amino acids, and antioxidants, plus a high-powered B complex. Designed by Nisha to help girls get exactly what they need day to day. Delivered in a delicious citrus or berry powder that mixes in water for quick absorption.

Weight-Loss Supplements
Weekly weight-loss packets—daily packets for weight-loss support and health
Chromium picolinate—blood sugar balance
L-carnitine—energy and focus
Fat burners—natural support for metabolism
Essential fatty acids/flaxseed oil—great for healthy skin, brain, hair, and heart
Thyroid-stimulating supplements—natural botanicals for supporting weak thyroid
Fat-burning protein shakes
Fat-burning protein bars

Products for Treating PMS
Full-spectrum light—for those who have problems with Seasonal Affective Disorder
Teen Balance for PMS—herbal supplements for support
Evening primrose oil—natural hormone balancer
Progesterone cream—natural plant-based cream for topical use
5-HTP supplement—raises serotonin for mood support

Products for Treating Insomnia
Sleep formula—natural, non-habit-forming capsules
Calcium/magnesium—helpful for calming and relaxing
GABA—to curb anxiety and restlessness
Melatonin drops (sublingual)
5-HTP supplement
Valerian root

TEEN/MOM QUESTIONNAIRE

Want to start a conversation with your daughter about how her life differs from yours when you were her age? Copy this questionnaire and either fill it out separately and compare answers later, or simply go through the questions together over a cup of tea and jot down mother and daughter responses side by side. This exercise is guaranteed to spark meaningful dialogue.

Moms substitute "did" for "do," etc.
One extra question for moms: What year were you the same age as your daughter is now?

1. How many hours do you spend in classes each school day?

2. How many hours do you average a week doing homework?

3. Do you have your own cell phone?

4. How many minutes do you talk on the phone per day, including cell phone and a home phone that is shared by the family?

5. Do you have access to a home computer?

6. How many hours do you spend on the computer per day?

7. How many hours do you spend per day watching television, including regular shows, video games, movies, news, etc.?

8. How many extracurricular activities are you involved in, including sports, clubs, youth groups, teams, music lessons, etc.?

9. How many hours per week do you average on those activities?

10. Do you have an after-school job? If so, how many hours do you work each week?

11. How many evenings per week do you spend at home with your family?

12. How many hours of sleep do you average per night?

13. What is your typical weekday bedtime?

14. How many hours per week do you spend doing chores around the home?

15. How many evenings per week do you eat dinner at home with the family?

16. How many hours do you spend with friends per week?

17. How many times per week do you eat out, including fast-food and sit-down restaurants, mall meals, or convenience store quick bites? Include lunches in your tally.

18. How many days per week do you eat breakfast?

19. What do you typically eat for breakfast?

20. Do you have one day each week that is typically spent in relaxing activities?

21. What is your favorite snack?

22. At what age did you start your period?

23. At what age did you have your first date?

24. Do you feel as if your weight is a problem?

25. Are any of your friends sexually active?

26. What percentage of the girls in your school do you estimate are sexually active?

27. What is your favorite free-time activity?

28. Do you regularly attend a church or religious service?

29. How many days per month do you feel emotionally down, have the "blues," or feel depressed?

30. On a scale of 1 to 10 how do you rate your everyday stress level, with 1 being no stress and 10 being extreme stress?

GLOSSARY

5-HTP, a supplement that acts as a precursor to the neurotransmitter serotonin; has been shown to be an effective supplement in the treatment of PMS, depression, insomnia, and weight control.

acne vulgaris, the medical term for common acne, which is characterized by the presence of one or more of the following: blackheads, whiteheads, papules, or pustules.

adolescence, the state of having reached puberty but not adulthood.

androgens, a class of sex hormones associated with the development and maintenance of secondary sex characteristics and sexual differentiation. In addition to increasing sexual function and libido, they stimulate skeletal growth.

anorexia, an eating disorder characterized by markedly reduced appetite or total aversion to food. Anorexia is a serious psychological disorder. The affected person, most often a girl or young woman, continues the endless cycle of restrictive eating, often to a point close to starvation. Anorexia can be life-threatening. Also called *anorexia nervosa.*

aphrodisiacs, substances that enhance sexual desire, or are thought to enhance sexual desire.

bioflavonoids, any of a group of biologically active substances found in plants and functioning in the maintenance of the walls of small blood vessels in mammals.

bioidentical hormones, compounds that are formulated to be molecularly identical to the hormones produced by the body.

bulimia, an eating disorder characterized by episodes of secretive excessive eating (bingeing) followed by inappropriate methods of weight control, such as self-induced vomiting (purging), abuse of laxatives and diuretics, and excessive exercise. Like anorexia, bulimia is a psychological disorder that goes beyond dieting.

CBC, stands for *complete blood count.*

cervix, refers to the neck of the womb.

circadian rhythm, the "body clock" that regulates our sleep pattern; it tells us when to sleep, awaken, have a bowel movement, and be at our peak performance. Also regulates specific hormones in the body.

corpus luteum, a yellow mass of tissue that forms in part of the ovary (graafian follicle) after ovulation and secretes the hormone progesterone.

cortisol, the stress hormone. Produced by the adrenal system in response to stress that can exert great influence on the nervous system, blood pressure, pulse rate, metabolism, and fat storage.

Day 1, the first day of the menstruation period.

diabetes mellitus, a disorder in which the pancreas produces insufficient or no insulin, the hormone responsible for the absorption of glucose. There are two main types of diabetes mellitus. Insulin-dependent (type 1) usually first appears under age thirty-five and most often between the ages of ten and sixteen. Without regular injections of insulin, the sufferer will slip into a coma and die. Noninsulin dependent diabetes (type 2) usually occurs gradually in people over age forty. Today it is becoming more common in young people, including children and teens, as their rates of obesity increase.

endometriosis, a condition in which tissue from the lining of the uterus, or similar tissue resembling the lining, occurs in various locations in the pelvic cavity, outside the uterine walls.

endometrium, the mucous membrane lining of the uterus.

endorphin, a morphinelike substance that alleviates pain and contributes to feelings of improved self-esteem, euphoria, and emotional well-being. The feel-good brain chemicals that are released during exercise; they counterbalance the ill effects of headaches.

EPO, stands for *evening primrose oil.*

estradiol, the most potent of the estrogens and the one in greatest evidence in premenopausal women. Produced by fertile ovaries.

estriol, the weakest form of the estrogens; it is at its highest levels during pregnancy. Produced from the conversion of estrone.

estrogen, the key female sex hormone responsible for the development and maintenance of female reproductive organs, especially breast and uterus, and the secondary sex characteristics, such as distribution of fat and hair patterns. Three types of estrogen are produced by the ovaries, and, to a lesser extent, by the adrenal glands: *estradiol, estrone,* and *estriol.*

estrogen dominance, the condition in which a female's estrogen levels may be low, normal, or excessive, but she has little or no progesterone to balance the effects of estrogen on the body. Symptoms include weight gain, fibrocystic breasts, fibroid uterine tumors, unstable emotions, irritability, acne, and bloating. Common teen menstrual irregularities such as heavy periods, cramping, or missed periods can also result.

estrone, an estrogen produced from the conversion of estradiol in the fat cells. The dominant estrogen after menopause; associated with fat storage.

evening primrose oil (EPO), a supplement available in capsule form that can be effective for treating PMS.

fallopian tube, a duct that transports ovum (eggs) from the ovary to the uterus.

fibrocystic breast disease, benign breast disease that presents as tiny, painful breast lumps that come and go with the cycle; closely related to estrogen and progesterone balance.

fibroids, benign smooth muscle tumors of the uterus that may cause vaginal bleeding and increased uterine cramping. The size of fibroids is driven largely by estrogen levels in the body.

follicle, a small secretory sac or cavity that surrounds ovum (eggs) in the ovary.

follicular phase, the preovulatory phase of the menstrual cycle, during which the egg grows inside the follicle and high estrogen levels build up the uterine lining. Days 1 to 13 of the cycle. See also *proliferative phase.*

FSH, stands for *follicle-stimulating hormone.* Produced by the pituitary gland in the brain and stimulates the development and release of mature eggs from ovarian follicles. Stimulates ovarian cells to secrete estrogens.

g, stands for *gram.*

hormone, a chemical substance produced by an organ, endocrine glands, or special cells, that is carried through the bloodstream to exert a regulatory or stimulatory effect on the activity of certain organs or bodily processes, such as metabolism.

hormone panel, comprehensive test that measures a female's levels of estrogen, progesterone, testosterone, DHEA (dehydroepiandrosterone), and thyroid hormones.

hyperthyroidism, excessive functional activity of the thyroid gland, resulting in an overproduction of thyroid hormones.

hypothyroidism, a condition resulting from underproduction of thyroid hormones from the thyroid glands, also known as *underactive thyroid.* Affects more women than men, and the risk increases with age for both. Symptoms include cold hands and feet, emotional disturbances, extreme fatigue, and constipation.

insulin, a hormone produced by the pancreas in varying amounts depending on the level of blood glucose (sugar). Carbohydrates are absorbed as glucose, increasing the blood glucose level and stimulating the pancreas to produce insulin. Insulin promotes the absorption of glucose into the liver, where it is stored as glycogen to be used later for exertion or in response to stress; or into muscle cells, where it is converted into energy.

insulin resistance, a condition in which the body doesn't respond to insulin properly. It is often linked to obesity, hypertension, and a diet that is high in sugar and other refined carbohydrates that prompt the body to overproduce insulin. Insulin resistance is part of the *metabolic syndrome* and a precursor to diabetes mellitus.

isoflavones, a type of phytoestrogen (derived from plants) that has weak estrogenic activity. Isoflavones possess myriad biological properties that can affect many physiological processes and may help create a more balanced hormonal state. Isoflavones are found in some legumes and are most concentrated in soy.

IU, stands for *international units.*

LH, stands for *lutenizing hormone,* which stimulates the ovary to release mature ova and prepares the uterus for the implantation of a fertilized egg. It also stimulates the formation of the corpus luteum in the ovaries.

luteal phase, the postovulatory phase of the menstrual cycle; the time in which progesterone is predominantly produced, causing the uterine lining to secrete substances that support the implantation of the embryo. Days 14 to 28 of the cycle.

mcg, stands for *microgram.*

mg, stands for *milligram.*

melatonin, the light-sensitive, sleep-regulating hormone produced by the pineal gland.

menarche, refers to the onset of menstruation. This occurs at puberty and can be anywhere between the ages of ten and seventeen, depending on the individual.

menopause, the termination of the menstrual cycle in women in midlife between the ages of forty and fifty-five years.

menstruation or menstrual phase, the phase of the menstrual cycle during which blood, tissue, mucus, and fluid is discharged from the lining of the uterus (endometrium), that usually lasts from three to five days. It is caused by a sudden reduction in estrogen and progesterone. The first day of flow is considered day 1 of the menstrual cycle.

metabolic syndrome, a group of conditions that place people at high risk for coronary artery disease. These conditions include type 2 diabetes, obesity, high blood pressure, and a poor lipid profile with elevated LDL ("bad") cholesterol, low HDL ("good") cholesterol, and elevated triglycerides. All of these conditions are associated with high blood insulin levels. The primary defect in the metabolic syndrome is insulin resistance.

mittelschmerz, pain in the area of the ovary that is felt at the time of ovulation (usually midway through the menstrual cycle).

natural hormones, hormones synthesized from plants that are bioidentical in molecular structure to those made by the human body. They have the same effect as the body's own hormones and do not interfere with the body's own hormone production.

ng/dl, stands for *nanograms per deciliter.*

NSAID, a nonsteroidal anti-inflammatory drug, such as aspirin or ibuprofen.

osteoporosis, a disease in which the bones become extremely porous, are subject to fracture, and heal slowly; occurs especially in women past menopause but may also occur in younger women with certain eating disorders.

ovary, female gland that produces hormones and the female reproductive or germ cell (ova).

ovulation, the release, typically between days 12 and 14 of the menstrual cycle, of a fertile ovum or egg from the ovary into the fallopian tube.

ovum (plural) or **ova** (singular)**,** the female reproductive egg or germ cell.

PCOS, see *polycystic ovary syndrome.*

pg/ml, stands for *picograms per milliliter.*

phytoestrogens, plant hormones.

pituitary gland, a gland located in the brain that regulates a wide range of bodily activities from growth to reproduction.

PMS, see *premenstrual syndrome.*

polycystic ovary syndrome (PCOS), a condition characterized by irregular or no menstrual periods, acne, obesity, excess body hair growth, and numerous small ovarian cysts. PCOS is a disorder of chronically abnormal ovarian function and abnormally elevated androgen levels. It affects 5 to 10 percent of females of reproductive age and increases the risk for high blood pressure, diabetes, heart disease, and cancer of the uterus. Much of this risk can be reversed by exercise and weight loss.

premenstrual syndrome, commonly known as *PMS*. Condition that includes physical and psychological/emotional symptoms associated with the later phase of the menstrual cycle. It is usually followed by a period of time that is symptom-free. Mood-related symptoms include irritability, depression, and fatigue. Physical symptoms include headaches, food cravings, water retention, breast tenderness, acne, hives, cold sores, herpes outbreaks, asthma, throat or gland swelling, seizures, recurrent yeast or bladder infections, and flu-like symptoms.

progesterone, a hormone produced in the second half of the menstrual cycle after ovulation; works with estrogen to prepare the uterus for conception.

progestin, a synthetic version of progesterone, made in the laboratory and chemically different from progesterone produced by the body.

proliferative phase, the phase of the menstrual cycle following menstruation, during which the pituitary gland, under the effect of FSH (follicle-stimulating hormone) from the ovary, makes estrogen, causing the lining of the uterus to thicken. The end of the proliferative phase is with the release of the egg (ovulation). See also *follicular phase.*

prostaglandins, any of a group of hormonelike substances produced in various tissues that are derived from amino acids and mediate a range of physiological functions, such as metabolism and nerve transmission.

puberty, the stage of becoming physiologically capable of sexual reproduction, marked by genital maturation, development of sexual characteristics, and, in girls, the first occurrence of menstruation.

SAD, stands for *seasonal affective disorder.*

saliva test, a salivary analysis of the hormone profile.

seasonal affective disorder (SAD), psychological disorder caused by a lack of sunlight. Treated with full-spectrum light therapy.

sebaceous glands, glands in the skin that produce an oily substance called sebum—these glands are the sites of acne lesions. Sebaceous glands are attached to hair follicles and are found mostly on the face, neck, back, and chest.

sebum, the oily substance produced by sebaceous glands.

secretory phase, the second half of the menstrual cycle after ovulation; the corpus luteum secretes progesterone, which prepares the endometrium for the implantation of an embryo; if fertilization does not occur, menstrual flow will begin. See also *luteal phase.*

serotonin, a powerful brain chemical that is thought to regulate mood, libido, appetite, and sleep. It is produced by the brain and body from the amino acid tryptophan, which is found in such foods as red meat, dairy products, nuts, seeds, bananas, soybeans and soy products, tuna, shellfish, and turkey.

serum (blood) test, drawing small amounts of blood to measure levels of various blood-borne substances, including hormones.

sex hormones, male and female hormones produced by the ovaries, testicles, adrenal glands, and body fat: estrogens, progesterone, androgens, and testosterone.

steroid hormones, cortisol, DHEA, estrogen, progesterone, and testosterone.

testosterone, present in both males and females, it is produced in small amounts by the ovaries and adrenal glands. It is a vital hormone that women need for energy, vitality, sex drive, and endurance.

topical, on the skin.

toxic stress, a condition in which a person is under excessive and prolonged stress; the body churns out a poisonous level of stress hormones, which is too much to withstand on a day-to-day basis.

urine hormone test, a type of lab test that uses the urine to analyze hormone levels in the body.

uterus, hollow, muscular organ in females that is the site of menstruation, implantation, development of the fetus, and labor. Also called the *womb*.

xenohormones, chemical elements from outside the human body that exert unnatural hormonelike effects inside the body. Xenohormones have been implicated in various cancers, early puberty, and other abnormalities and illnesses.